EINKORN FLOUR COOKBOOK

The Clean-Eating Baking Guide to Simple, Gut-Friendly Recipes. Crafted with the world's oldest grain, cherished for its simplicity and nutrition

Elina Rowley

© 2025 The Ultimate Fresh-Milled Einkorn Flour Cookbook All rights reserved.

This document is intended exclusively for informational purposes and pertains solely to 'The Ultimate Fresh-Milled Einkorn Flour Cookbook.' The book is provided "as is," with no guarantees, either express or implied.

Unauthorized reproduction, distribution, or transmission of any part of this book is strictly forbidden. The publisher disclaims all liability for any damages arising from the use or misuse of the information contained herein.

All trademarks and brand names mentioned within this book are the property of their respective owners.

TABLE OF CONTENTS

CHAPTER 1: INTRODUCTION … 6
- History and Characteristics of Einkorn … 6
- Advantages of Fresh-Milled Flour … 6
  - Nutritional Superiority of Fresh-Milled Einkorn … 7
- Einkorn's Unique Flavor and Texture … 7
- Milling Your Own Flour at Home … 8
  - Essential Equipment and Milling Techniques … 9
  - Proper Storage for Freshness and Quality … 10

CHAPTER 2: 20 BREAKFAST RECIPES … 11
1. Einkorn Blueberry Pancakes … 11
2. Savory Einkorn Breakfast Muffins … 12
3. Einkorn Cinnamon Rolls … 13
4. Einkorn Banana Nut Bread … 14
5. Einkorn Waffles with Maple Syrup … 15
6. Fresh-Milled Einkorn Crepes … 16
7. Einkorn Sourdough English Muffins … 17
8. Einkorn Granola Parfait … 18
9. Einkorn Apple Cinnamon Scones … 19
10. Einkorn Breakfast Biscotti … 20
11. Einkorn Zucchini Bread … 21
12. Einkorn French Toast … 22
13. Einkorn Breakfast Casserole … 23
14. Einkorn Chia Seed Pudding … 24
15. Einkorn Breakfast Pizza … 25
16. Einkorn Quiche with Spinach … 26
17. Einkorn Breakfast Burritos … 27
18. Einkorn Bagels with Cream Cheese … 28
19. Einkorn Breakfast Bars … 29
20. Einkorn Lemon Poppy Seed Muffins … 30

CHAPTER 3: 20 BREAD RECIPES … 31
21. Einkorn Artisan Sourdough … 31
22. Einkorn Whole Wheat Sandwich Bread … 32
23. Einkorn Honey Oat Bread … 33
24. Einkorn Rosemary Focaccia … 34
25. Einkorn Garlic Herb Breadsticks … 35
26. Einkorn Multigrain Loaf … 36
27. Einkorn Olive Bread … 37
28. Einkorn Pita Bread … 38
29. Einkorn Rye Bread … 39
30. Einkorn Brioche … 40
31. Einkorn Flatbread … 41
32. Einkorn Pull-Apart Rolls … 42
33. Einkorn Pumpkin Bread … 43
34. Einkorn Challah … 44
35. Einkorn Ciabatta … 45
36. Einkorn Pretzel Rolls … 46
37. Einkorn Naan … 47
38. Einkorn Country Loaf … 48
39. Einkorn Seeded Bread … 49
40. Einkorn Baguette … 50

CHAPTER 4: 20 DESSERT RECIPES … 51
41. Einkorn Chocolate Chip Cookies … 51
42. Einkorn Lemon Bars … 52
43. Einkorn Brownies … 53
44. Einkorn Carrot Cake … 54
45. Einkorn Apple Pie … 55
46. Einkorn Chocolate Cake … 56
47. Einkorn Cheesecake … 57
48. Einkorn Peanut Butter Cookies … 58

49. Einkorn Cinnamon Coffee Cake	59		82. Einkorn Fettuccine Alfredo	92
50. Einkorn Berry Tart	60		83. Einkorn Linguine with Clam Sauce	93
51. Einkorn Chocolate Mousse	61		84. Einkorn Pesto Pasta	94
52. Einkorn Pumpkin Pie	62		85. Einkorn Lasagna	95
53. Einkorn Lemon Pound Cake	63		86. Einkorn Macaroni and Cheese	96
54. Einkorn Linzer Cookies	64		87. Einkorn Pad Thai	97
55. Einkorn Coconut Macaroons	65		88. Einkorn Ramen Noodle Soup	98
56. Einkorn Shortbread Cookies	66		89. Einkorn Udon Noodles with Soy Sauce	99
57. Einkorn Pecan Pie	67		90. Einkorn Penne Arrabbiata	100
58. Einkorn Strawberry Shortcake	68		91. Einkorn Sesame Noodles	101
59. Einkorn Chocolate Eclairs	69		92. Einkorn Carbonara	102
60. Einkorn Banana Cream Pie	70		93. Einkorn Gnocchi with Marinara Sauce	103

CHAPTER 5: 20 SAVORY SNACKS   71

61. Einkorn Cheese Crackers	71
62. Einkorn Herb Crackers	72
63. Einkorn Pretzel Bites	73
64. Einkorn Parmesan Breadsticks	74
65. Einkorn Spinach and Feta Puffs	75
66. Einkorn Garlic Knots	76
67. Einkorn Jalapeño Cornbread Muffins	77
68. Einkorn Onion Rings	78
69. Einkorn Savory Hand Pies	79
70. Einkorn Cheddar Scones	80
71. Einkorn Savory Pinwheels	81
72. Einkorn Tomato Basil Tartlets	82
73. Einkorn Stuffed Breadsticks	83
74. Einkorn Olive Tapenade Rolls	84
75. Einkorn Zucchini Fritters	85
76. Einkorn Herb and Cheese Biscuits	86
77. Einkorn Spicy Bread Twists	87
78. Einkorn Stuffed Mushrooms	88
79. Einkorn Vegetable Empanadas	89
80. Einkorn Savory Scones	90

CHAPTER 6: PASTA AND NOODLE RECIPES   91

81. Einkorn Spaghetti with Garlic and Olive Oil   91

94. Einkorn Ravioli with Spinach and Ricotta   104

95. Einkorn Lo Mein	105
96. Einkorn Ziti with Sausage and Peppers	106
97. Einkorn Orzo Salad	107
98. Einkorn Tortellini Soup	108
99. Einkorn Pho	109
100. Einkorn Chow Mein	110

CHAPTER 7: EXPERTISE IN DOUGH HANDLING   111

Kneading Techniques for Einkorn Dough	111
Troubleshooting Dough Disasters	111
Common Dough Preparation Mistakes	112
Achieving the Ideal Rise in Einkorn Dough	112

CHAPTER 8: NUTRITIONAL INSIGHTS OF EINKORN   113

Einkorn Flour in a Balanced Diet	113
Dietary Considerations for Einkorn Flour	114
Gluten Content in Einkorn	114
Gluten Sensitivity and Einkorn	115

CHAPTER 9: EXPERT EINKORN COOKING TIPS   115

Enhancing Einkorn Flavor Profiles	115
Substituting Einkorn in Traditional Recipes	116

CHAPTER 10: CREATIVE BLENDS WITH EINKORN FLOUR   117

    Mixing Einkorn with Other Ancient Grains   117

    Flavorful Einkorn and Grain Combinations 118

Texture and Density with Einkorn Blends   118

Chapter 1: Introduction

History and Characteristics of Einkorn

Einkorn, scientifically known as **Triticum monococcum**, is one of the oldest types of cultivated wheat, with signs of its domestication going back over 10,000 years. Unlike modern wheat varieties that have been heavily hybridized and altered to improve yield and disease resistance, einkorn has kept much of its original genetic makeup. This ancient cereal grain was an important part of the diet for early farming societies and has been found at many archaeological sites in the Fertile Crescent, a region known as the birthplace of agriculture. Its strong nature and ability to grow in poor soil, without needing chemical fertilizers or advanced farming methods, made it a vital crop for early farming communities.

Einkorn has unique features that set it apart from both modern wheat and other ancient grains. The kernels of einkorn are smaller and longer compared to those of today's wheat species. Each grain is covered in a tightly stuck husk, which means it needs to be hulled after harvest to get to the edible part. This husk helps protect the grain from pests and diseases, reducing the need for chemical pesticides and fungicides. Einkorn flour is well-liked for its rich, nutty flavor and its beautiful golden color, which adds a depth of taste to baked goods that is often missing in products made from modern wheat flour.

Nutritionally, einkorn provides better benefits than modern wheat, with more protein, phosphorus, vitamin B6, and beta-carotene. It is also a good source of dietary antioxidants, including lutein, which is important for eye health. The gluten structure in einkorn is simpler and less cross-linked, which may make it easier to digest for those who are sensitive to gluten in modern wheat. However, it is still not safe for people with celiac disease because it contains gluten proteins.

Today, einkorn is seeing a comeback, especially among small farmers and organic producers. This revival is fueled by a growing interest in traditional grains and a focus on sustainable farming practices. Freshly milled einkorn flour, made from grinding the whole grain kernels, keeps all the nutritional benefits and rich flavor of the grain. This is in contrast to the commercial milling of modern wheat, where the nutritious bran and germ are often removed, leading to a loss in nutritional value.

When used in baking, einkorn flour behaves quite differently from modern wheat flour, mainly due to its lower gluten content and unique gluten structure. It absorbs less liquid, resulting in stickier doughs that need careful handling during preparation. These traits require changes to usual baking methods, such as adjusting how much water is used and using gentler kneading techniques, to get the right texture and structure in the finished baked goods.

Advantages of Fresh-Milled Flour

Fresh-milled einkorn flour offers many benefits for cooking and baking, greatly improving the nutrition, taste, and texture of your dishes. One major advantage is the freshness of the flour. Unlike store-bought flours, which can sit on shelves for a long time, fresh-milled flour keeps all its natural oils, vitamins, and minerals. This is important because these components give the flour a richer taste and more nutrients. Fresh milling means these elements don't break down or lose their quality, which often happens with flours that have been stored for a while. As a result, baked goods made with fresh-milled flour have a more complex and layered flavor, especially in bread, pastries, and other recipes where flour is key.

The digestibility of fresh-milled einkorn flour is better because of its unique gluten structure. Einkorn, an ancient grain, has a simpler gluten structure compared to the more complex gluten found in modern wheat. This simplicity makes it easier to digest for many people, especially those with mild gluten sensitivities, who might feel discomfort with highly processed flours. The gluten in einkorn is lighter and less dense, leading to a gentler digestive experience. However, it's important to note that einkorn still contains gluten, so it is not suitable for people with celiac disease, who need to avoid gluten completely.

Choosing fresh-milled einkorn flour also has positive effects on the environment, especially when it comes from local farmers or is milled at home. Einkorn grows well in less fertile soil and doesn't need synthetic fertilizers or pesticides, making it a more eco-friendly option. This grain's ability to thrive in tough conditions helps reduce the environmental impact of its growing process. Supporting einkorn farming also helps smaller farms, which are more likely to use traditional and sustainable farming methods, promoting biodiversity and decreasing dependence on industrial farming.

Milling einkorn flour at home gives you the benefit of customization, allowing you to control the texture of the flour. You can adjust the milling process to create flour with different coarseness, suited to various baking needs. For example, a coarser grind is better for rustic bread and certain pastries, adding a hearty texture, while a finer grind works well for cakes and delicate baked goods that need a soft crumb. This ability to customize the milling process helps bakers achieve the perfect texture and crumb structure in their recipes.

The nutritional advantages of fresh-milled einkorn flour make a strong case for including it in your diet. Einkorn has more essential nutrients than modern wheat, providing higher amounts of protein, phosphorus, vitamin B6, and the antioxidant lutein. These nutrients are important for various health aspects, from supporting muscle function to promoting eye health. Fresh milling helps keep these nutrients intact, unlike commercially milled flours that often remove the bran and germ, leading to a big loss in nutrition.

Nutritional Superiority of Fresh-Milled Einkorn

Einkorn flour, especially when freshly milled, is highly valued for its strong nutritional benefits, making it a popular choice for health-conscious people aged 25 to 50. This group often enjoys cooking and baking and looks for ingredients that are not only healthy but also tasty and have a good texture. Freshly milled einkorn flour is a nutrient-rich alternative to regular flours, keeping its full range of vitamins, minerals, and helpful plant compounds that are often lost in commercial flour processing.

One of the standout features of einkorn flour is its higher protein content, which is essential for many body functions. Protein is key for building and repairing tissues, making enzymes and hormones, and maintaining overall health. Einkorn flour has more protein than modern wheat flours, making it especially beneficial for those focused on muscle maintenance and growth. This is particularly important for people looking to boost their protein intake from plant sources, as einkorn offers a strong option to meet their dietary needs.

In addition to protein, einkorn flour is a great source of essential minerals like phosphorus, magnesium, and zinc. Phosphorus is important for healthy bones and teeth, helping with protein synthesis and energy storage through adenosine triphosphate (ATP). Magnesium is vital for muscle and nerve function, controlling blood sugar levels, and maintaining healthy blood pressure. Zinc is crucial for a strong immune system, wound healing, DNA synthesis, and cell division. Together, these minerals support many body functions and overall health.

Einkorn flour also has several B vitamins, especially vitamin B6, which helps support the immune system, aids in protein metabolism, and is involved in red blood cell production. Adding einkorn flour to your diet can help ensure you get enough of these important nutrients, which can help maintain energy levels and overall health.

The antioxidant properties of einkorn flour, particularly from its lutein content—a carotenoid linked to eye health—are another notable benefit. Antioxidants protect the body from damage caused by free radicals, increasing the nutritional value of the flour and offering protective benefits against chronic diseases.

The structure of gluten in einkorn flour is simpler compared to modern wheat, which may make it easier to digest for people with mild gluten sensitivities. However, it is still not suitable for those with celiac disease. This better digestibility, along with its rich nutrient profile, makes einkorn flour an attractive choice for those looking to boost their digestive health while enjoying the versatility of baked goods and other flour-based recipes.

Einkorn's Unique Flavor and Texture

Einkorn flour, with its rich history, brings a unique flavor and texture that makes it different from modern wheat flours. Its flavor often combines nutty, earthy, and lightly sweet notes, which greatly enhance the taste of baked goods. This special flavor comes from the grain's genetic traits, which have stayed mostly the same over thousands of years, and from the specific environment where it is grown. The grain's ability to take in various minerals from the soil adds to its deep flavor. When einkorn flour is freshly milled, it keeps all its natural oils and nutrients, boosting its nutritional value and intensifying its flavors. This richness makes einkorn perfect for recipes where flour is important, adding a complexity and depth that refined flours often lack.

The texture of einkorn flour is also noteworthy. Because it has less gluten and a different structure of gluten proteins, einkorn flour creates doughs and batters that are less stretchy and more delicate than those made with regular wheat flour. This means you need to handle the mixing and kneading gently to avoid making the dough too tough or dense. When handled properly, einkorn flour can result in baked goods with a soft crumb and a pleasing chewiness, making it great for artisan breads, light pastries, and other treats where a tender texture is key.

For bakers new to einkorn's special traits, adjusting the amount of liquid in recipes is very important. Einkorn absorbs liquid differently and usually needs less than recipes using modern wheat flour. It's best to start with a smaller amount of liquid and gradually add more, watching the dough closely to get the right consistency. This is crucial to avoid creating overly wet or sticky doughs, which can be hard to work with.

Working with einkorn dough requires a careful and patient approach. The way einkorn dough ferments is different from regular wheat doughs because of its simpler gluten structure, which ferments more slowly. Letting the dough rise slowly, often in a cooler spot, can greatly improve both its flavor and texture. This slow fermentation helps develop a richer flavor and contributes to a better texture in the final baked goods.

Milling Your Own Flour at Home

Milling your own einkorn flour at home gives you all the nutritional benefits and unique flavor of this ancient grain, making your baking experience special. The first step is to get a home grain mill, which can be electric or manual. Electric grain mills are quick and easy to use, often featuring different speed settings and motor strengths to handle various grains well. They are perfect for those who want speed and convenience, with some models able to produce fine flour in just a few minutes. On the other hand, manual grain mills need some physical effort to operate, usually using a hand crank. This can make the milling process more engaging and hands-on. These mills tend to be more affordable and have fewer parts that can wear out, making them a sturdy choice for budget-conscious bakers or those who like a more traditional approach. Here is a guide on how to mill einkorn flour at home:

1. **Select Einkorn Wheat Berries**: Choose high-quality, organic einkorn wheat berries to ensure the best flour. When selecting, check the berries for even size and color, making sure they are free from stones, chaff, or other grains that could affect the flavor and nutrients of the flour. Consider where the einkorn wheat berries come from, as different regions may add subtle flavor differences.

2. **Prepare Your Grain Mill**: Before you start milling, read the operational instructions from your grain mill's manufacturer. Each model may have special features that you need to understand. Adjust the mill's settings to get the flour coarseness you want by changing the space between the grinding stones or burrs. For cakes and pastries, you'll want a finer flour, so set it closer together. For bread and rustic goods, a coarser grind is better, giving a heartier texture and flavor.

3. **Mill the Einkorn Wheat Berries**: Start milling by adding a measured amount of einkorn wheat berries into the mill's hopper. If you're using an electric mill, be sure to set the right speed to avoid overheating, which can lower the flour's quality and change its taste. Keep a close eye on the milling process to ensure a consistent output, adjusting settings as needed to maintain the desired flour texture.

4. **Sift the Flour (Optional)**: If you want a finer flour texture, sifting can help remove larger bran pieces for a smoother consistency. This step is based on your baking preferences and the recipe's needs. Using a fine-mesh sieve or a special flour sifter can help you get the right level of smoothness.

5. **Store Your Fresh-Milled Einkorn Flour**: To keep the best flavor and nutrients of freshly milled flour, use it soon after milling. If you need to store it, put the flour in an airtight container to protect it from moisture and air, which can spoil it. Refrigerating or freezing is a good way to extend its shelf life, and remember to label the container with the milling date to keep track of freshness.

6. **Adjust Your Recipes**: When using freshly milled einkorn flour in your recipes, you'll need to change the liquid amounts. Einkorn flour has a different gluten structure and absorbs liquid differently compared to store-bought flours. Start with less liquid than the recipe calls for, and gradually add more until you reach the right dough

consistency. This adjustment is key to getting the best texture and structure in your baked goods.

7. **Experiment and Adjust**: Because home-milled flour can vary slightly in texture and moisture, it's important to be flexible with your recipes. Pay attention to the dough's feel and consistency. Try out different baking techniques to improve your skills and find the best ingredient balance that works with your home-milled einkorn flour.

Essential Equipment and Milling Techniques

To start milling your own einkorn flour at home, you need the right equipment designed for this ancient grain. This section covers the essential tools and methods needed to create high-quality flour that keeps the nutritional benefits and unique taste of einkorn.

Essential Equipment for Home Milling

1. **Grain Mill**: A reliable grain mill is key for successful home milling, and there are two main types: **electric** and **manual**. Electric mills are made for speed and efficiency, with many models that can create everything from coarse to very fine flour. It's important to choose a model with adjustable settings so you can control the flour's texture. These settings usually adjust the distance between the grinding stones or burrs, which affects how the flour turns out. On the other hand, manual mills require some physical effort, offering a hands-on experience that some people enjoy. They are often made from strong materials, making them durable and a good value.

2. **Scales**: Using a digital kitchen scale is vital for accurate measurements of einkorn wheat berries before milling and for checking the flour yield afterward. This accuracy is important to ensure your baking recipes turn out consistently, as even small weight differences can affect the results.

3. **Sifter**: A fine-mesh sifter or sieve helps you achieve a smoother flour texture. This process involves sifting the freshly milled flour to remove larger bran pieces, which is especially useful for recipes that need a lighter flour.

4. **Storage Containers**: To keep freshly milled flour fresh, airtight storage containers are necessary. These containers protect the flour from moisture and air. It's best to choose containers that seal well and are made from materials like glass or food-grade plastic that won't change the flour's flavor.

Effective Milling Techniques

1. **Preparation**: Before milling, check that the einkorn wheat berries are free of stones or debris that could damage the mill. If you've stored the wheat berries in a cool place, letting them warm to room temperature can help the milling process go more smoothly.

2. **Milling Settings**: Adjusting the grain mill settings is an important step that affects the final flour texture. For finer flour, the grinding stones or burrs should be closer together. Start with a coarser setting to see how the mill works, then adjust as needed for your desired texture. Keep in mind that making finer flour may take longer, especially with manual mills.

3. **Milling in Batches**: To avoid overheating, especially with electric models, it's best to mill in smaller batches. Overheating can reduce flour quality and harm the mill. If needed, let the mill cool between batches.

4. **Monitoring the Flour**: Keep an eye on the flour while milling to ensure a consistent texture. If you spot any large bits or uneven milling, adjust the settings. For electric mills, listen for any changes in the motor's sound, which can indicate that adjustments are needed.

5. **Post-Milling Sifting**: Sifting the flour through a fine-mesh sieve after milling can help achieve a uniform texture. While this step is optional, it depends on your personal preference and the recipe's needs.

6. **Immediate Use or Storage**: To enjoy the best flavor and nutritional value of fresh-milled einkorn flour, try to use it soon after milling. For storage, move the flour to an airtight container, label it with the milling date, and keep it in a cool, dark place. If you plan to store it for a long time, refrigeration or freezing is a good idea to maintain quality.

7. **Recipe Adjustments**: When using home-milled einkorn flour in recipes, remember to adjust the liquid amounts. Freshly milled flour absorbs liquid differently than store-bought flour. It's wise to start with less liquid than the recipe calls for, adding more as needed until you reach the right consistency.

Proper Storage for Freshness and Quality

To ensure the best preservation of freshly milled einkorn flour, careful storage practices are very important. Unlike store-bought flour, freshly milled flour doesn't have synthetic preservatives, making it more likely to spoil quickly. Use these techniques to keep the flour's nutritional benefits and unique taste:

1. **Airtight Containers**: Right after milling, move the einkorn flour into airtight containers. Oxygen can speed up reactions that break down important nutrients like vitamin E and cause unpleasant flavors. Choose containers made from non-reactive materials like glass or stainless steel, and make sure the lids fit tightly to create a seal. These materials are great because they don't mix with or hold onto smells, which helps keep the flour pure. Also, keeping out moisture is crucial to prevent mold, which can grow even in low humidity.

2. **Cool, Dark Storage**: Store the flour in a cool place away from light. Light and heat can damage sensitive vitamins like thiamine and riboflavin and can affect the good fats in the flour. Find a spot like a pantry or cabinet that is not exposed to direct sunlight and away from heat sources like ovens and refrigerators to avoid unwanted heat.

3. **Refrigeration for Longevity**: If you plan to store the flour for a while, refrigeration is a smart choice. A cooler temperature slows down the breakdown process and helps prevent bacteria and mold. Make sure the container is sealed well to keep out any odors from the fridge that could change the flour's taste. In the fridge, the flour can stay fresh for several months.

4. **Freezing for Maximum Freshness**: For the longest storage time, freezing the freshly milled einkorn flour is the best method. Use containers or bags made for the freezer, ensuring they are airtight to avoid freezer burn and moisture. Clearly label each container with the milling date to keep track of what you have. Before using the flour, let it come to room temperature to prevent moisture from forming, which could affect its texture and how it bakes.

5. **Vacuum Sealing**: Use a vacuum sealer to remove air from the storage bags, which slows down the breakdown process and helps the flour last longer. This method is especially useful for those who mill large amounts of flour but use it gradually. By taking out the oxygen, vacuum sealing helps keep the flour's nutrients and flavor for a longer time.

6. **Regular Inspection**: Check the stored flour regularly for signs of spoilage. Smell for any bad odors, look for clumping, and check for mold to ensure the flour is still good. Keeping the flour fresh is key for great baking results and to maximize its health benefits.

Chapter 2: 20 Breakfast Recipes

1. Einkorn Blueberry Pancakes

Number of servings: 4

Preparation time: 15 minutes

Cooking time: 10 minutes

Ingredients:

- 1 cup fresh-milled einkorn flour
- 1 tablespoon sugar
- 1 teaspoon baking powder
- 1/2 teaspoon salt
- 1 egg, beaten
- 1 cup milk (any kind works, but almond milk is a great alternative)
- 2 tablespoons unsalted butter, melted, plus more for greasing the pan
- 1/2 teaspoon vanilla extract
- 1 cup fresh blueberries
- Optional: Maple syrup and extra blueberries for serving

Directions:

1. In a large mixing bowl, whisk together the einkorn flour, sugar, baking powder, and salt.

2. In another bowl, mix the beaten egg, milk, melted butter, and vanilla extract until well combined.

3. Pour the wet ingredients into the dry ingredients. Stir until just combined; it's okay if there are a few lumps. Do not overmix.

4. Gently fold in the blueberries.

5. Heat a non-stick skillet or griddle over medium heat and brush with a little butter.

6. Pour 1/4 cup of batter for each pancake onto the skillet. Cook until bubbles form on the surface, about 2-3 minutes, then flip and cook for another 2 minutes or until golden brown.

7. Serve warm with maple syrup and extra blueberries, if desired.

Nutritional value per serving:

- Calories: 235
- Carbs: 36g
- Fiber: 4g
- Sugars: 10g
- Protein: 6g
- Saturated fat: 3g
- Unsaturated fat: 2g

Difficulty rating: Easy

Tips for ingredient variations:

- For a dairy-free version, use almond milk and a plant-based butter alternative.
- Add a pinch of cinnamon or nutmeg to the batter for a spiced flavor.
- Substitute blueberries with other berries or chocolate chips for a different twist.

2. Savory Einkorn Breakfast Muffins

Number of servings: 12 muffins

Preparation time: 20 minutes

Cooking time: 25 minutes

Ingredients:

- 2 cups fresh-milled einkorn flour
- 1 tablespoon baking powder
- 1/2 teaspoon salt
- 1/4 teaspoon black pepper
- 1 cup grated cheddar cheese
- 1/2 cup finely chopped spinach
- 1/4 cup sun-dried tomatoes, chopped
- 1/4 cup fresh basil, chopped
- 2 large eggs
- 1 cup whole milk
- 1/4 cup olive oil
- 1/4 cup unsalted butter, melted

Directions:

1. Preheat your oven to 375°F (190°C). Grease a 12-cup muffin tin or line with paper muffin cups.

2. In a large mixing bowl, whisk together the fresh-milled einkorn flour, baking powder, salt, and black pepper.

3. Stir in the grated cheddar cheese, chopped spinach, sun-dried tomatoes, and fresh basil until they are evenly distributed throughout the flour mixture.

4. In a separate bowl, beat the eggs lightly, then mix in the whole milk, olive oil, and melted butter until well combined.

5. Pour the wet ingredients into the dry ingredients. Stir until just combined; be careful not to overmix.

6. Spoon the batter into the prepared muffin cups, filling each about three-quarters full.

7. Bake in the preheated oven for 25 minutes, or until the tops are golden and a toothpick inserted into the center of a muffin comes out clean.

8. Remove the muffins from the oven and let them cool in the pan for 5 minutes before transferring them to a wire rack to cool completely.

Nutritional value per serving:

- Calories: 210
- Carbs: 18g
- Fiber: 2g
- Sugars: 2g
- Protein: 7g
- Saturated fat: 5g
- Unsaturated fat: 3g

Difficulty rating: Easy

Tips for ingredient variations:

- Swap out the cheddar cheese for any cheese you prefer, such as feta for a tangier taste or mozzarella for a milder flavor.

- Feel free to replace spinach with kale or any other leafy greens you have on hand.

- For a meatier version, add cooked and crumbled bacon or sausage to the batter.

- If you're looking for a bit more crunch, throw in a handful of chopped nuts like walnuts or pecans.

3. Einkorn Cinnamon Rolls

Number of servings: 12 rolls

Preparation time: 2 hours

Cooking time: 25 minutes

Ingredients:

- For the dough:
  - 4 cups fresh-milled einkorn flour
  - 1 cup warm milk
  - 1/2 cup granulated sugar
  - 2 1/4 teaspoons active dry yeast (1 packet)
  - 1/3 cup unsalted butter, melted
  - 2 large eggs
  - 1 teaspoon salt
- For the filling:
  - 1 cup brown sugar, packed
  - 3 tablespoons ground cinnamon
  - 1/3 cup unsalted butter, softened
- For the frosting:
  - 6 ounces cream cheese, softened
  - 1/3 cup unsalted butter, softened
  - 2 cups powdered sugar
  - 1 teaspoon vanilla extract
  - 1-2 tablespoons milk (as needed for consistency)

Directions:

1. In a large mixing bowl, combine warm milk, granulated sugar, and yeast. Let it sit for 5-10 minutes until the mixture is frothy.

2. Add the melted butter, eggs, and salt to the yeast mixture. Gradually mix in the einkorn flour until the dough begins to form.

3. Transfer the dough to a floured surface and knead for about 5 minutes, or until smooth and elastic. Einkorn dough will be slightly stickier than traditional wheat dough; avoid adding too much flour.

4. Place the dough in a greased bowl, cover with a clean towel, and let it rise in a warm place for about 1 hour, or until doubled in size.

5. While the dough is rising, prepare the filling by mixing the brown sugar and cinnamon in a bowl.

6. Preheat your oven to 350°F (175°C) and grease a 9x13 inch baking pan.

7. Once the dough has risen, roll it out on a floured surface into a 16x21 inch rectangle. Spread the softened butter over the dough, then sprinkle evenly with the cinnamon-sugar mixture.

8. Roll the dough tightly from the long end, and cut into 12 equal pieces using a sharp knife or dental floss.

9. Place the rolls in the prepared baking pan, cover, and let them rise again for 30 minutes.

10. Bake in the preheated oven for 25 minutes, or until golden brown.

11. While the rolls are baking, prepare the frosting by beating together the cream cheese, butter, powdered sugar, and vanilla extract. Add milk as needed to achieve a smooth, spreadable consistency. Remove the rolls from the oven and allow them to cool slightly before spreading the frosting on top.

Nutritional value per serving: Calories: 450, Carbs: 68g, Fiber: 2g, Sugars: 42g, Protein: 6g, Saturated fat: 15g, Unsaturated fat: 3g

Difficulty rating: Medium

Tips for ingredient variations:

- For a dairy-free version, substitute the milk with almond milk, the butter with coconut oil, and use a dairy-free cream cheese alternative for the frosting.

4. Einkorn Banana Nut Bread

Number of servings: 1 loaf (8-10 slices)

Preparation time: 20 minutes

Cooking time: 55 minutes

Ingredients:

- 2 cups fresh-milled einkorn flour
- 1 teaspoon baking soda
- 1/4 teaspoon salt
- 1/2 cup unsalted butter, at room temperature
- 3/4 cup brown sugar
- 2 large eggs, beaten
- 2 1/3 cups mashed overripe bananas (about 4-5 medium bananas)
- 1 teaspoon vanilla extract
- 1/2 cup chopped walnuts (optional)

Directions:

1. Preheat your oven to 350°F (175°C). Grease a 9x5 inch loaf pan.

2. In a small bowl, whisk together the fresh-milled einkorn flour, baking soda, and salt. Set aside.

3. In a large bowl, cream the butter and brown sugar together until light and fluffy. Add the beaten eggs, mashed bananas, and vanilla extract, mixing until well combined.

4. Gradually add the dry ingredients to the wet ingredients, stirring just until the flour is incorporated. Avoid overmixing.

5. Fold in the chopped walnuts, if using.

6. Pour the batter into the prepared loaf pan and smooth the top with a spatula.

7. Bake in the preheated oven for 55 minutes, or until a toothpick inserted into the center comes out clean.

8. Let the bread cool in the pan for 10 minutes, then turn out onto a wire rack to cool completely.

Nutritional value per serving (per slice, based on 10 slices per loaf):

- Calories: 230
- Carbs: 33g
- Fiber: 2g
- Sugars: 16g
- Protein: 4g
- Saturated fat: 5g
- Unsaturated fat: 3g

Difficulty rating: Easy

Tips for ingredient variations:

- For a nut-free version, omit the walnuts or replace them with the same amount of chocolate chips or dried fruit such as cranberries or raisins.

- To enhance the flavor, consider adding 1/2 teaspoon of cinnamon or nutmeg to the dry ingredients.

- For a vegan version, substitute the butter with coconut oil and use flax eggs (1 flax egg = 1 tablespoon ground flaxseed mixed with 3 tablespoons water, let sit for 15 minutes) instead of regular eggs.

5. Einkorn Waffles with Maple Syrup

Number of servings: 4

Preparation time: 15 minutes

Cooking time: 20 minutes

Ingredients:

- 2 cups fresh-milled einkorn flour
- 2 teaspoons baking powder
- 1/2 teaspoon salt
- 2 tablespoons sugar
- 2 large eggs
- 1 1/2 cups whole milk
- 1/3 cup unsalted butter, melted
- 1 teaspoon vanilla extract
- Maple syrup, for serving

Directions:

1. Preheat your waffle iron according to the manufacturer's instructions.

2. In a large mixing bowl, whisk together the einkorn flour, baking powder, salt, and sugar.

3. In a separate bowl, beat the eggs and then mix in the milk, melted butter, and vanilla extract.

4. Pour the wet ingredients into the dry ingredients and stir until just combined. Be careful not to overmix; a few lumps are okay.

5. Grease the waffle iron with a little butter or cooking spray. Pour enough batter into the iron to just cover the waffle grid.

6. Close the lid and cook until the waffle is golden and crisp. This will take about 4-5 minutes, but follow your waffle iron's instructions.

7. Carefully remove the waffle and serve immediately with maple syrup.

Nutritional value per serving:

- Calories: 450
- Carbs: 58g
- Fiber: 4g
- Sugars: 12g
- Protein: 12g
- Saturated fat: 10g
- Unsaturated fat: 5g

Difficulty rating: Easy

Tips for ingredient variations:

- For a dairy-free version, substitute the whole milk with almond milk and use a plant-based butter.

- Add a half cup of fresh blueberries or chocolate chips to the batter for extra flavor.

- For a healthier twist, reduce the sugar to 1 tablespoon and serve with fresh fruit instead of syrup.

6. Fresh-Milled Einkorn Crepes

Number of servings: 4

Preparation time: 15 minutes

Cooking time: 20 minutes

Ingredients:

- 1 cup fresh-milled einkorn flour
- 2 large eggs
- 1 1/2 cups whole milk
- 1/4 teaspoon salt
- 2 tablespoons unsalted butter, melted, plus more for cooking
- 1 teaspoon pure vanilla extract (optional for sweet crepes)
- Powdered sugar, fresh berries, and maple syrup for serving (optional for sweet crepes)

Directions:

1. In a large mixing bowl, whisk together the einkorn flour and salt.

2. In another bowl, beat the eggs, then mix in the milk, melted butter, and vanilla extract if making sweet crepes.

3. Gradually add the wet ingredients to the dry ingredients, whisking continuously until the batter is smooth and free of lumps. Let the batter rest for 5 minutes to allow the einkorn flour to fully hydrate.

4. Heat a non-stick skillet or crepe pan over medium heat. Brush the pan lightly with melted butter.

5. Pour about 1/4 cup of batter into the center of the pan, tilting and swirling the pan immediately to spread the batter thinly across the bottom.

6. Cook for about 1-2 minutes, or until the edges of the crepe begin to lightly brown and lift from the pan. Use a spatula to flip the crepe gently and cook for another 30 seconds to 1 minute on the other side.

7. Transfer the cooked crepe to a plate and cover with a kitchen towel to keep warm. Repeat with the remaining batter, adding more butter to the pan as needed.

8. Serve the crepes warm, with powdered sugar, fresh berries, and maple syrup if desired.

Nutritional value per serving (for plain crepes without toppings):

- Calories: 210
- Carbs: 22g
- Fiber: 2g
- Sugars: 3g
- Protein: 8g
- Saturated fat: 5g
- Unsaturated fat: 3g

Difficulty rating: Easy

Tips for ingredient variations:

- For savory crepes, omit the vanilla extract and serve with fillings such as sautéed vegetables, cheese, and cooked meats.

- Experiment with adding herbs or spices to the batter for savory crepes, such as chopped fresh chives or a pinch of cayenne pepper.

- For a dairy-free version, substitute the whole milk with almond milk and use a dairy-free butter alternative.

7. Einkorn Sourdough English Muffins

Number of servings: 8 muffins

Preparation time: 20 minutes

Cooking time: 10 minutes per batch

Ingredients:

- 1 cup fresh-milled einkorn flour
- 1 teaspoon baking powder
- 1/2 teaspoon salt
- 1 tablespoon sugar
- 1 cup sourdough starter, active and bubbly
- 1/4 cup milk (any kind, including dairy-free alternatives)
- 2 tablespoons unsalted butter, melted (or a plant-based alternative)
- Cornmeal, for dusting

Directions:

1. In a large mixing bowl, whisk together the fresh-milled einkorn flour, baking powder, salt, and sugar.

2. In a separate bowl, combine the sourdough starter, milk, and melted butter.

3. Pour the wet ingredients into the dry ingredients. Stir until just combined; the batter should be slightly sticky but manageable.

4. Dust a clean surface with cornmeal. Turn out the dough onto the surface and gently pat it into a thickness of about 1/2 inch.

5. Using a round cutter or a glass, cut out muffins from the dough. Re-knead and cut the scraps until all the dough is used.

6. Preheat a skillet or griddle over medium-low heat. Dust lightly with cornmeal.

7. Place the muffins in the skillet, ensuring they are not touching. Cook for about 5 minutes on each side or until they are golden brown and cooked through.

8. Transfer the cooked muffins to a wire rack to cool slightly. Serve warm.

Nutritional value per serving:

- Calories: 150
- Carbs: 28g
- Fiber: 4g
- Sugars: 3g
- Protein: 5g
- Saturated fat: 1.5g
- Unsaturated fat: 1g

Difficulty rating: Medium

Tips for ingredient variations:

- For a dairy-free version, use any plant-based milk and a plant-based butter alternative.

- Add 1/2 teaspoon of cinnamon or vanilla extract to the batter for a sweet twist.

- For a savory option, mix in 1/4 cup of grated cheese and 1 tablespoon of chopped fresh herbs into the batter before cooking.

8. Einkorn Granola Parfait

Number of servings: 4

Preparation time: 15 minutes

Cooking time: 20 minutes

Ingredients:

- 2 cups fresh-milled einkorn flour
- 1/4 cup honey
- 1/4 cup coconut oil, melted
- 1/2 teaspoon salt
- 1 teaspoon cinnamon
- 1/2 cup almonds, chopped
- 1/2 cup dried cranberries
- 2 cups Greek yogurt
- 1 cup fresh berries (strawberries, blueberries, raspberries, or a mix)
- 4 tablespoons honey (for layering)

Directions:

1. Preheat your oven to 325°F (163°C) and line a baking sheet with parchment paper.

2. In a large bowl, combine the fresh-milled einkorn flour, 1/4 cup honey, melted coconut oil, salt, and cinnamon. Mix until all ingredients are well incorporated.

3. Spread the mixture evenly on the prepared baking sheet and bake for 10 minutes.

4. Remove from the oven, stir in the chopped almonds, and bake for an additional 10 minutes or until the granola is lightly golden.

5. Let the granola cool completely on the baking sheet. Once cooled, break it apart and mix in the dried cranberries.

6. To assemble the parfaits, layer 1/2 cup of Greek yogurt at the bottom of each serving glass, followed by a layer of granola, then a drizzle of honey, and finally a layer of fresh berries.

7. Repeat the layering process until the glasses are filled, finishing with a layer of berries on top.

Nutritional value per serving:

- Calories: 450
- Carbs: 60g
- Fiber: 8g
- Sugars: 35g
- Protein: 15g
- Saturated fat: 8g
- Unsaturated fat: 5g

Difficulty rating: Easy

Tips for ingredient variations:

- Substitute almonds with any other nuts like walnuts or pecans for a different flavor profile.

- Feel free to use maple syrup instead of honey for a vegan option.

- Mix in other dried fruits such as apricots or figs in place of cranberries for variety.

- For a dairy-free version, substitute Greek yogurt with coconut yogurt or another plant-based yogurt.

9. Einkorn Apple Cinnamon Scones

Number of servings: 8 scones

Preparation time: 20 minutes

Cooking time: 25 minutes

Ingredients:

- 2 cups fresh-milled einkorn flour
- 1/3 cup granulated sugar
- 1 tablespoon baking powder
- 1/2 teaspoon salt
- 1 teaspoon ground cinnamon
- 1/2 cup cold unsalted butter, cut into small pieces
- 3/4 cup heavy cream, plus more for brushing
- 1 large egg
- 1 teaspoon vanilla extract
- 1 cup diced apples (about 1 medium apple)
- 2 tablespoons raw sugar, for sprinkling

Directions:

1. Preheat your oven to 400°F (200°C) and line a baking sheet with parchment paper.

2. In a large mixing bowl, whisk together the fresh-milled einkorn flour, granulated sugar, baking powder, salt, and ground cinnamon.

3. Add the cold butter pieces to the flour mixture. Using a pastry cutter or your fingertips, work the butter into the flour until the mixture resembles coarse crumbs.

4. In a separate bowl, whisk together the heavy cream, egg, and vanilla extract. Pour this wet mixture into the flour and butter mixture, stirring just until combined. Do not overmix.

5. Gently fold in the diced apples until evenly distributed throughout the dough.

6. Turn the dough out onto a lightly floured surface and shape it into a round disk about 1 inch thick. Using a sharp knife, cut the disk into 8 equal wedges.

7. Place the scone wedges on the prepared baking sheet, leaving space between each one. Brush the tops of the scones with a little extra heavy cream and sprinkle with raw sugar.

8. Bake in the preheated oven for 25 minutes, or until the scones are golden brown and a toothpick inserted into the center comes out clean.

9. Remove from the oven and let cool on the baking sheet for 5 minutes before transferring to a wire rack to cool completely.

Nutritional value per serving (1 scone): Calories: 345, Carbs: 39g, Fiber: 2g, Sugars: 16g, Protein: 5g, Saturated fat: 11g, Unsaturated fat: 3g

Difficulty rating: Medium

Tips for ingredient variations:

- For a healthier version, substitute the granulated sugar with coconut sugar and the heavy cream with coconut cream.

- Feel free to add nuts such as walnuts or pecans to the dough for added texture and flavor.

- Swap out the apples for pears or mix in some dried cranberries for a different twist on this classic recipe.

10. Einkorn Breakfast Biscotti

Number of servings: 24 biscotti

Preparation time: 20 minutes

Cooking time: 50 minutes

Ingredients:

- 2 cups fresh-milled einkorn flour
- 1 teaspoon baking powder
- 1/4 teaspoon salt
- 3/4 cup cane sugar
- 3 large eggs
- 1 teaspoon vanilla extract
- 1/2 cup almonds, roughly chopped
- 1/2 cup dried cranberries

Directions:

1. Preheat your oven to 350°F (175°C) and line a baking sheet with parchment paper.

2. In a large bowl, whisk together the fresh-milled einkorn flour, baking powder, and salt.

3. In a separate bowl, beat the sugar and eggs until light and fluffy, about 3-4 minutes. Mix in the vanilla extract.

4. Gradually add the dry ingredients to the egg mixture, stirring until just combined.

5. Fold in the chopped almonds and dried cranberries.

6. Divide the dough in half and form two logs approximately 12 inches long and 2 inches wide on the prepared baking sheet.

7. Bake for 30 minutes, or until the logs are lightly browned.

8. Remove from the oven and let cool for 10 minutes. Reduce the oven temperature to 300°F (150°C).

9. Transfer the logs to a cutting board and slice diagonally into 1/2 inch thick slices using a serrated knife.

10. Place the biscotti cut side down on the baking sheet and bake for an additional 20 minutes, turning halfway through, until they are crisp.

11. Let the biscotti cool completely on a wire rack before serving.

Nutritional value per serving: Calories: 100, Carbs: 15g, Fiber: 1g, Sugars: 8g, Protein: 2g, Saturated fat: 0.5g, Unsaturated fat: 1g

Difficulty rating: Medium

Tips for ingredient variations:

- Substitute almonds with pecans or walnuts for a different nutty flavor.

- Dried cherries or apricots can be used in place of cranberries for a tart twist.

- For a chocolatey version, add 1/2 cup of dark chocolate chips to the dough.

11. Einkorn Zucchini Bread

Number of servings: 1 loaf (about 12 slices)

Preparation time: 20 minutes

Cooking time: 60 minutes

Ingredients:

- 2 cups fresh-milled einkorn flour
- 1 teaspoon baking powder
- 1/2 teaspoon baking soda
- 1/2 teaspoon salt
- 1 teaspoon ground cinnamon
- 1/2 cup unsalted butter, melted
- 3/4 cup granulated sugar
- 2 large eggs
- 1 teaspoon vanilla extract
- 1 1/2 cups grated zucchini (about 1 medium zucchini)
- 1/2 cup chopped walnuts (optional)

Directions:

1. Preheat your oven to 350°F (175°C). Grease a 9x5 inch loaf pan and set aside.

2. In a large bowl, whisk together the fresh-milled einkorn flour, baking powder, baking soda, salt, and cinnamon.

3. In a separate bowl, mix the melted butter and sugar until well combined. Beat in the eggs, one at a time, then stir in the vanilla extract.

4. Gradually add the wet ingredients to the dry ingredients, stirring until just combined. Do not overmix.

5. Fold in the grated zucchini and walnuts (if using) until evenly distributed throughout the batter.

6. Pour the batter into the prepared loaf pan and smooth the top with a spatula.

7. Bake in the preheated oven for 60 minutes, or until a toothpick inserted into the center comes out clean.

8. Allow the bread to cool in the pan for 10 minutes, then transfer to a wire rack to cool completely before slicing.

Nutritional value per serving (1 slice):

- Calories: 210
- Carbs: 29g
- Fiber: 2g
- Sugars: 15g
- Protein: 4g
- Saturated fat: 5g
- Unsaturated fat: 3g

Difficulty rating: Easy

Tips for ingredient variations:

- For a healthier version, substitute the granulated sugar with coconut sugar or a sugar alternative of your choice. Adjust the amount to taste.

- Add 1/2 cup of raisins or dried cranberries for extra sweetness and texture.

- For a vegan option, replace the eggs with flax eggs (1 flax egg = 1 tablespoon ground flaxseed + 3 tablespoons water) and use a plant-based butter substitute.

12. Einkorn French Toast

Number of servings: 4

Preparation time: 15 minutes

Cooking time: 10 minutes

Ingredients:

- 8 slices of thick-cut bread (preferably stale, for better absorption)
- 1 cup fresh-milled einkorn flour
- 1 cup whole milk
- 4 large eggs
- 2 tablespoons granulated sugar
- 1 teaspoon vanilla extract
- 1/2 teaspoon ground cinnamon
- Pinch of salt
- Butter, for frying
- Maple syrup, for serving
- Fresh berries (optional), for serving

Directions:

1. In a large mixing bowl, whisk together the fresh-milled einkorn flour, milk, eggs, granulated sugar, vanilla extract, ground cinnamon, and a pinch of salt until well combined and smooth.

2. Heat a large skillet or griddle over medium heat and add a small amount of butter to coat the surface.

3. Dip each slice of bread into the einkorn mixture, allowing it to soak for a few seconds on each side. Ensure both sides are well coated but not overly soggy.

4. Place the soaked bread slices onto the heated skillet and cook for about 2-3 minutes on each side, or until golden brown and slightly crispy.

5. Repeat with the remaining bread slices, adding more butter to the skillet as needed.

6. Serve the einkorn French toast warm, topped with maple syrup and fresh berries, if desired.

Nutritional value per serving (1 serving = 2 slices):

- Calories: 350
- Carbs: 45g
- Fiber: 4g
- Sugars: 12g
- Protein: 14g
- Saturated fat: 5g
- Unsaturated fat: 3g

Difficulty rating: Easy

Tips for ingredient variations:

- For a dairy-free version, substitute almond milk or coconut milk for whole milk.

- If you prefer a sweeter French toast, increase the granulated sugar to 3 tablespoons or add a tablespoon of maple syrup to the batter.

- Experiment with toppings like nut butter, yogurt, or a sprinkle of powdered sugar for added flavor and texture.

13. Einkorn Breakfast Casserole

Number of servings: 8

Preparation time: 20 minutes

Cooking time: 45 minutes

Ingredients:

- 1 tablespoon olive oil
- 1 medium onion, diced
- 1 red bell pepper, diced
- 1 pound breakfast sausage (pork or turkey)
- 2 cups fresh spinach, roughly chopped
- 6 large eggs
- 1 cup whole milk
- 1/2 teaspoon salt
- 1/4 teaspoon black pepper
- 1 cup shredded cheddar cheese
- 1 cup fresh-milled einkorn flour
- 1 teaspoon baking powder

Directions:

1. Preheat your oven to 350°F (175°C). Grease a 9x13 inch baking dish with butter or non-stick spray.

2. Heat olive oil in a large skillet over medium heat. Add the diced onion and bell pepper, sautéing until softened, about 5 minutes.

3. Add the breakfast sausage to the skillet, breaking it apart with a spoon. Cook until no longer pink, about 7 minutes. Stir in the chopped spinach and cook until wilted, approximately 2 minutes. Remove from heat and set aside.

4. In a large mixing bowl, whisk together eggs, milk, salt, and pepper until well combined.

5. In a separate bowl, mix the fresh-milled einkorn flour with baking powder.

6. Gradually add the flour mixture to the egg mixture, stirring until just combined.

7. Spread the sausage and vegetable mixture evenly in the bottom of the prepared baking dish.

8. Sprinkle half of the shredded cheese over the sausage mixture.

9. Pour the egg and flour mixture over the cheese layer, using a spatula to spread evenly if necessary.

10. Top with the remaining cheese.

11. Bake in the preheated oven for 35-45 minutes, or until the casserole is set in the middle and the cheese is golden brown.

12. Let the casserole cool for 5 minutes before slicing and serving.

Nutritional value per serving:

- Calories: 350
- Carbs: 18g
- Fiber: 2g
- Sugars: 3g
- Protein: 22g
- Saturated fat: 9g
- Unsaturated fat: 5g

Difficulty rating: Medium

Tips for ingredient variations:

- For a vegetarian version, omit the sausage and add an additional cup of vegetables such as mushrooms or zucchini.

- Swap out cheddar cheese for any cheese of your choice, such as mozzarella or pepper jack, for a different flavor profile.

- Add herbs such as chives, parsley, or dill to the egg mixture for added freshness and flavor.

14. Einkorn Chia Seed Pudding

Number of servings: 4

Preparation time: 15 minutes

Cooking time: 0 minutes (Requires at least 4 hours of refrigeration)

Ingredients:

- 1/4 cup fresh-milled einkorn flour
- 2 tablespoons chia seeds
- 1 cup unsweetened almond milk (or any milk of choice)
- 2 tablespoons pure maple syrup
- 1/2 teaspoon pure vanilla extract
- Pinch of salt
- Fresh berries and nuts for topping (optional)

Directions:

1. In a medium mixing bowl, whisk together the fresh-milled einkorn flour and chia seeds.

2. Add the almond milk, maple syrup, vanilla extract, and a pinch of salt to the bowl. Whisk until well combined and the mixture begins to thicken.

3. Cover the bowl with a lid or plastic wrap and refrigerate for at least 4 hours, or overnight. This allows the chia seeds to absorb the liquid and thicken the pudding.

4. Before serving, stir the pudding well. If the pudding is too thick, you can add a little more milk until you reach your desired consistency.

5. Serve the chia seed pudding in bowls or glasses, topped with fresh berries and nuts if desired.

Nutritional value per serving (without toppings): Calories: 150, Carbs: 20g, Fiber: 4g, Sugars: 8g, Protein: 3g, Saturated fat: 0.5g, Unsaturated fat: 2g

Difficulty rating: Easy

Tips for ingredient variations:

- For a chocolate version, add 1 tablespoon of cocoa powder to the mixture before refrigerating.

- Sweeten the pudding with honey or agave syrup instead of maple syrup if preferred.

- Experiment with different milks such as coconut milk, soy milk, or cow's milk to find your favorite flavor and consistency.

- Add a tablespoon of peanut butter or almond butter for a nutty flavor.

- Incorporate spices such as cinnamon or nutmeg for added warmth and depth.

15. Einkorn Breakfast Pizza

Number of servings: 4

Preparation time: 20 minutes

Cooking time: 15 minutes

Ingredients:

- 1 cup fresh-milled einkorn flour
- 1 teaspoon instant yeast
- 1/2 teaspoon salt
- 1/2 cup warm water
- 1 tablespoon olive oil, plus extra for greasing
- 1/2 cup tomato sauce
- 1 cup shredded mozzarella cheese
- 1/2 cup cooked and crumbled breakfast sausage
- 1/4 cup sliced bell peppers
- 1/4 cup sliced red onions
- 4 eggs
- Salt and pepper, to taste
- Fresh basil leaves, for garnish

Directions:

1. In a mixing bowl, combine the einkorn flour, instant yeast, and salt. Add the warm water and 1 tablespoon of olive oil, and mix until a dough forms.

2. Knead the dough on a floured surface for about 5 minutes, until smooth. Place in a greased bowl, cover, and let rise for 1 hour.

3. Preheat your oven to 475°F (245°C). Grease a pizza pan or baking sheet with olive oil.

4. Roll out the dough on a floured surface to form a 12-inch circle. Transfer to the prepared pizza pan.

5. Spread the tomato sauce evenly over the dough, leaving a small border around the edges. Sprinkle the shredded mozzarella cheese on top of the sauce.

6. Distribute the cooked sausage, bell peppers, and red onions evenly over the cheese.

7. Make four wells in the toppings and crack an egg into each well. Season with salt and pepper.

8. Bake in the preheated oven for 12-15 minutes, or until the crust is golden brown and the eggs are set to your liking.

9. Garnish with fresh basil leaves before serving.

Nutritional value per serving: Calories: 350, Carbs: 30g, Fiber: 4g, Sugars: 3g, Protein: 20g, Saturated fat: 5g, Unsaturated fat: 3g

Difficulty rating: Medium

Tips for ingredient variations:

- For a vegetarian option, omit the sausage and add mushrooms or spinach.

- Feel free to substitute the mozzarella with any cheese of your choice, such as cheddar or feta.

- Add a spicy kick by including sliced jalapeños or a drizzle of hot sauce on top before baking.

16. Einkorn Quiche with Spinach

Number of servings: 6

Preparation time: 25 minutes

Cooking time: 35 minutes

Ingredients:

- 1 cup fresh-milled einkorn flour
- 1/4 teaspoon salt
- 6 tablespoons unsalted butter, chilled and cubed
- 2-4 tablespoons ice water
- 1 tablespoon olive oil
- 1 small onion, finely chopped
- 2 cups fresh spinach, roughly chopped
- 4 large eggs
- 1 cup heavy cream
- 1/2 cup grated Gruyère cheese
- 1/4 teaspoon nutmeg
- Salt and pepper to taste

Directions:

1. Preheat your oven to 375°F (190°C).

2. In a large bowl, combine einkorn flour and salt. Add the cubed butter and use your fingers or a pastry cutter to blend until the mixture resembles coarse crumbs.

3. Gradually add ice water, 1 tablespoon at a time, mixing until the dough just comes together. Form into a disk, wrap in plastic, and chill for at least 30 minutes.

4. On a floured surface, roll out the dough into a 12-inch circle. Transfer to a 9-inch pie dish, gently pressing into the bottom and sides. Trim any excess dough from the edges.

5. In a skillet over medium heat, heat the olive oil. Add the onion and cook until translucent, about 5 minutes. Add the spinach and cook until wilted, about 2 minutes. Remove from heat and let cool slightly.

6. In a bowl, whisk together eggs, heavy cream, nutmeg, salt, and pepper. Stir in the cooled spinach mixture and grated Gruyère.

7. Pour the filling into the prepared crust and smooth the top with a spatula.

8. Bake in the preheated oven until the filling is set and the crust is golden brown, about 35 minutes.

9. Let the quiche cool for 10 minutes before slicing and serving.

Nutritional value per serving:

- Calories: 435
- Carbs: 18g
- Fiber: 2g
- Sugars: 2g
- Protein: 12g
- Saturated fat: 18g
- Unsaturated fat: 8g

Difficulty rating: Medium

Tips for ingredient variations:

- Substitute spinach with kale or Swiss chard for a different flavor profile.
- For a lower fat option, use half-and-half instead of heavy cream.
- Add cooked bacon or ham to the filling for extra protein.
- Experiment with different cheeses such as cheddar or feta for a new taste.

17. Einkorn Breakfast Burritos

Number of servings: 4

Preparation time: 25 minutes

Cooking time: 15 minutes

Ingredients:

- 8 fresh-milled einkorn flour tortillas
- 8 large eggs
- 1/2 cup milk
- 1/4 teaspoon salt
- 1/4 teaspoon black pepper
- 1 cup shredded cheddar cheese
- 1 cup cooked and crumbled breakfast sausage
- 1/2 cup diced green bell pepper
- 1/2 cup diced red onion
- 1 tablespoon olive oil
- 1/2 cup salsa, for serving
- 1/4 cup chopped fresh cilantro, for garnish

Directions:

1. In a large bowl, whisk together eggs, milk, salt, and pepper until well combined.

2. Heat olive oil in a large skillet over medium heat. Add diced green bell pepper and red onion, sautéing until softened, about 3-4 minutes.

3. Pour the egg mixture into the skillet with the sautéed vegetables. Cook, stirring frequently, until the eggs are scrambled and fully cooked, approximately 5-6 minutes. Remove from heat.

4. Warm the einkorn flour tortillas in a separate skillet or microwave for 10-15 seconds to make them more pliable.

5. Lay out the warmed tortillas and evenly distribute the scrambled egg mixture among them.

6. Top each with cooked breakfast sausage and shredded cheddar cheese.

7. Roll up the tortillas to form burritos, folding in the sides to enclose the filling.

8. Serve each burrito with a side of salsa and garnish with chopped fresh cilantro.

Nutritional value per serving:

- Calories: 450
- Carbs: 38g
- Fiber: 4g
- Sugars: 3g
- Protein: 26g
- Saturated fat: 9g
- Unsaturated fat: 5g

Difficulty rating: Easy

Tips for ingredient variations:

- For a vegetarian option, substitute the breakfast sausage with sautéed mushrooms or spinach.

- Add a spicy kick by including diced jalapeños with the vegetables or using a spicy salsa as a topping.

- For a dairy-free version, omit the cheese or use a dairy-free cheese alternative.

18. Einkorn Bagels with Cream Cheese

Number of servings: 8 bagels

Preparation time: 2 hours

Cooking time: 25 minutes

Ingredients:

- 4 cups fresh-milled einkorn flour

- 1 tablespoon sugar

- 2 teaspoons salt

- 1 tablespoon instant yeast

- 1 1/2 cups warm water (about 110°F)

- 2 tablespoons olive oil

- 10 cups water (for boiling)

- 2 tablespoons honey (for boiling water)

- 1 egg white, beaten (for glaze)

- Optional toppings: sesame seeds, poppy seeds, minced garlic, or coarse salt

For serving:

- Cream cheese

Directions:

1. In a large mixing bowl, combine the einkorn flour, sugar, salt, and instant yeast.

2. Add the warm water and olive oil to the flour mixture. Mix until a dough forms.

3. Knead the dough on a lightly floured surface for about 10 minutes, or until it is smooth and elastic.

4. Place the dough in a greased bowl, covering it with a damp cloth. Let it rise in a warm place for 1 hour, or until it doubles in size.

5. Preheat your oven to 425°F (220°C). Line a baking sheet with parchment paper.

6. Bring the 10 cups of water to a boil in a large pot. Add the honey.

7. Punch down the dough and divide it into 8 equal pieces. Roll each piece into a ball, then use your thumb to make a hole in the center of each ball, stretching the dough to form a bagel shape.

8. Boil the bagels, a few at a time, in the honey water for 1 minute on each side.

9. Remove the bagels with a slotted spoon and place them on the prepared baking sheet.

10. Brush the top of each bagel with the beaten egg white and sprinkle with your choice of toppings.

11. Bake in the preheated oven for 20-25 minutes, or until golden brown.

12. Let the bagels cool on a wire rack before serving with cream cheese.

Nutritional value per serving (1 bagel without cream cheese): Calories: 260, Carbs: 48g, Fiber: 6g, Sugars: 3g, Protein: 9g, Saturated fat: 0.5g, Unsaturated fat: 2g

Difficulty rating: Medium

Tips for ingredient variations:

- For a sweeter bagel, add 1/4 cup of raisins or dried cranberries to the dough before the first rise.

- For a whole grain version, substitute 1 cup of the einkorn flour with fresh-milled einkorn whole grain flour.

- Experiment with different toppings like cinnamon sugar, dried onion flakes, or everything bagel seasoning for variety.

19. Einkorn Breakfast Bars

Number of servings: 12 bars

Preparation time: 15 minutes

Cooking time: 25 minutes

Ingredients:

- 2 cups fresh-milled einkorn flour
- 1 teaspoon baking powder
- 1/2 teaspoon salt
- 1/2 teaspoon cinnamon
- 1/4 cup coconut oil, melted
- 1/2 cup honey or maple syrup
- 1 egg
- 1 teaspoon vanilla extract
- 1/2 cup almond milk
- 1 cup mixed nuts and seeds (e.g., walnuts, almonds, pumpkin seeds)
- 1/2 cup dried fruits (e.g., cranberries, raisins)
- 1/4 cup dark chocolate chips (optional)

Directions:

1. Preheat your oven to 350°F (175°C). Line a 9x9 inch baking pan with parchment paper or lightly grease it.

2. In a large bowl, whisk together the fresh-milled einkorn flour, baking powder, salt, and cinnamon.

3. In a separate bowl, mix the melted coconut oil, honey (or maple syrup), egg, and vanilla extract until well combined.

4. Gradually add the wet ingredients to the dry ingredients, stirring until just combined. Avoid overmixing.

5. Stir in the almond milk to achieve a batter consistency. Fold in the mixed nuts, seeds, dried fruits, and dark chocolate chips, if using.

6. Spread the batter evenly into the prepared baking pan, smoothing the top with a spatula.

7. Bake for 25 minutes, or until the edges are golden brown and a toothpick inserted into the center comes out clean.

8. Allow the bars to cool in the pan for 10 minutes, then transfer to a wire rack to cool completely before cutting into bars.

Nutritional value per serving (1 bar):

- Calories: 210
- Carbs: 29g
- Fiber: 3g
- Sugars: 15g
- Protein: 5g
- Saturated fat: 4g
- Unsaturated fat: 3g

Difficulty rating: Easy

Tips for ingredient variations:

- For a nut-free version, substitute the mixed nuts with sunflower seeds or extra dried fruits.

- To make vegan, replace the egg with a flax egg (1 tablespoon ground flaxseed mixed with 3 tablespoons water, let sit for 15 minutes) and use maple syrup instead of honey.

- Feel free to customize the mix-ins based on your preferences or what you have on hand. Other great additions include shredded coconut, chia seeds, or a pinch of nutmeg for extra flavor.

20. Einkorn Lemon Poppy Seed Muffins

Number of servings: 12 muffins

Preparation time: 15 minutes

Cooking time: 20 minutes

Ingredients:

- 2 cups fresh-milled einkorn flour
- 3/4 cup granulated sugar
- 2 teaspoons baking powder
- 1/2 teaspoon salt
- 2 tablespoons poppy seeds
- Zest of 1 lemon
- 2 large eggs
- 1 cup whole milk
- 1/2 cup unsalted butter, melted
- 1/4 cup fresh lemon juice
- 1 teaspoon vanilla extract

Directions:

1. Preheat your oven to 375°F (190°C). Line a 12-cup muffin tin with paper liners or lightly grease with butter.

2. In a large mixing bowl, whisk together the einkorn flour, sugar, baking powder, salt, poppy seeds, and lemon zest.

3. In a separate bowl, beat the eggs lightly. Stir in the milk, melted butter, lemon juice, and vanilla extract until well combined.

4. Pour the wet ingredients into the dry ingredients. Gently fold together until just combined; be careful not to overmix.

5. Divide the batter evenly among the prepared muffin cups, filling each about 3/4 full.

6. Bake in the preheated oven for 20 minutes, or until a toothpick inserted into the center of a muffin comes out clean.

7. Allow the muffins to cool in the pan for 5 minutes before transferring them to a wire rack to cool completely.

Nutritional value per serving: (per muffin)

- Calories: 220
- Carbs: 29g
- Fiber: 1g
- Sugars: 15g
- Protein: 4g
- Saturated fat: 5g
- Unsaturated fat: 2g

Difficulty rating: Easy

Tips for ingredient variations:

- For a dairy-free version, substitute the whole milk with almond milk and use a plant-based butter alternative.

- If you prefer a less sweet muffin, reduce the sugar to 1/2 cup.

- Add a crunchy topping by sprinkling raw sugar and additional lemon zest over the muffins before baking.

- For an extra lemony flavor, increase the lemon zest to the zest of 2 lemons.

Chapter 3: 20 Bread Recipes

21. Einkorn Artisan Sourdough

Number of servings: 1 large loaf

Preparation time: 24 hours (including resting and proofing times)

Cooking time: 45 minutes

Ingredients:

- 1 cup active sourdough starter

- 3 cups fresh-milled einkorn flour, plus more for dusting

- 1 1/4 cups lukewarm water

- 1 teaspoon sea salt

Directions:

1. In a large mixing bowl, combine the sourdough starter, fresh-milled einkorn flour, and water. Mix until all ingredients are well incorporated. The dough will be sticky at this stage.

2. Cover the bowl with a damp cloth and let the dough rest for 30 minutes to allow the flour to fully hydrate.

3. Sprinkle the sea salt over the dough. Wet your hands to prevent sticking, and fold the dough over itself several times to incorporate the salt.

4. Cover the bowl again with the damp cloth and let the dough rise at room temperature for about 12 to 14 hours, or until roughly doubled in size.

5. After the first rise, lightly flour a work surface and your hands. Gently shape the dough into a round loaf without deflating it too much.

6. Place the shaped dough into a well-floured proofing basket or a bowl lined with a floured towel. Cover and let it rise for another 2 to 4 hours, or until it has visibly expanded and puffed up.

7. Approximately 30 minutes before baking, preheat your oven to 450°F (232°C) with a Dutch oven inside.

8. Carefully remove the hot Dutch oven from the preheated oven. Turn the proofing basket over to transfer the dough into the Dutch oven. Make a shallow slash across the top of the dough with a sharp knife or razor blade.

9. Cover the Dutch oven and bake for 20 minutes. After 20 minutes, remove the lid and continue baking for another 25 minutes, or until the loaf is golden brown and sounds hollow when tapped on the bottom.

10. Remove the loaf from the Dutch oven and let it cool on a wire rack for at least an hour before slicing.

Nutritional value per serving: (Based on the whole loaf)

- Calories: 1800

- Carbs: 360g

- Fiber: 48g

- Sugars: 0g

- Protein: 60g

- Saturated fat: 0g

- Unsaturated fat: 5g

Difficulty rating: Medium

Tips for ingredient variations:

- For a nuttier flavor, mix in 1/2 cup of toasted and chopped walnuts or pecans into the dough during the second fold.

- Incorporate 1/2 cup of dried cranberries or raisins for a sweet and tart contrast.

- Add 1 tablespoon of fresh rosemary or thyme to the dough for an aromatic twist.

22. Einkorn Whole Wheat Sandwich Bread

Number of servings: 1 loaf (about 12 slices)

Preparation time: 15 minutes

Cooking time: 40 minutes

Ingredients:

- 3 cups fresh-milled einkorn flour
- 1 cup warm water (about 110°F)
- 2 teaspoons instant yeast
- 1 teaspoon salt
- 2 tablespoons honey
- 2 tablespoons olive oil

Directions:

1. In a large mixing bowl, combine the warm water and honey, stirring until the honey is dissolved. Sprinkle the instant yeast over the water and let it sit for 5 minutes, or until it becomes frothy.

2. Add the fresh-milled einkorn flour and salt to the yeast mixture. Stir with a wooden spoon until a rough dough forms.

3. Drizzle the olive oil over the dough, then knead in the bowl for about 5 minutes. The dough should be slightly sticky but manageable. If it's too sticky, add a little more flour, one tablespoon at a time.

4. Transfer the dough to a lightly oiled bowl, turning it to coat all sides with oil. Cover the bowl with a clean kitchen towel and let the dough rise in a warm, draft-free place for about 1 hour, or until doubled in size.

5. Gently punch down the dough to release any air bubbles. Transfer the dough to a lightly floured surface and shape it into a loaf.

6. Place the shaped dough into a greased 9x5 inch loaf pan. Cover loosely with the kitchen towel and let it rise again for about 30 minutes, or until the dough has risen about 1 inch above the top of the pan.

7. Preheat your oven to 375°F (190°C).

8. Bake the bread in the preheated oven for 40 minutes, or until the top is golden brown and the loaf sounds hollow when tapped on the bottom.

9. Remove the bread from the oven and let it cool in the pan for 10 minutes. Then, transfer the loaf to a wire rack to cool completely before slicing.

Nutritional value per serving: (per slice, based on 12 slices per loaf)

- Calories: 150
- Carbs: 28g
- Fiber: 4g
- Sugars: 3g
- Protein: 4g
- Saturated fat: 0.5g
- Unsaturated fat: 1g

Difficulty rating: Easy

Tips for ingredient variations:

- For a sweeter loaf, increase the honey to 3 tablespoons.

- Add 1/2 cup of mix-ins like walnuts, sunflower seeds, or dried cranberries to the dough before the second rise for added texture and flavor.

- For a richer flavor, substitute the water with milk and increase the olive oil to 3 tablespoons.

23. Einkorn Honey Oat Bread

Number of servings: 1 loaf (about 12 slices)

Preparation time: 15 minutes

Cooking time: 50 minutes

Ingredients:

- 3 cups fresh-milled einkorn flour
- 1 cup rolled oats, plus extra for topping
- 1/4 cup honey
- 2 teaspoons baking powder
- 1/2 teaspoon baking soda
- 1/2 teaspoon salt
- 1 1/2 cups buttermilk
- 1/4 cup unsalted butter, melted
- 1 large egg

Directions:

1. Preheat your oven to 375°F (190°C). Grease a 9x5 inch loaf pan and sprinkle the bottom and sides with rolled oats.

2. In a large mixing bowl, combine the einkorn flour, 1 cup rolled oats, baking powder, baking soda, and salt.

3. In a separate bowl, whisk together the buttermilk, melted butter, honey, and egg until well blended.

4. Pour the wet ingredients into the dry ingredients. Stir until just combined; the batter will be slightly lumpy.

5. Transfer the batter into the prepared loaf pan. Smooth the top with a spatula and sprinkle with additional rolled oats.

6. Bake in the preheated oven for 50 minutes, or until a toothpick inserted into the center of the loaf comes out clean.

7. Remove from the oven and let the bread cool in the pan for 10 minutes. Then, transfer it to a wire rack to cool completely before slicing.

Nutritional value per serving: (per slice, based on 12 slices per loaf)

- Calories: 190
- Carbs: 32g
- Fiber: 3g
- Sugars: 7g
- Protein: 5g
- Saturated fat: 2g
- Unsaturated fat: 1g

Difficulty rating: Easy

Tips for ingredient variations:

- For a vegan version, substitute the buttermilk with almond milk mixed with 1 tablespoon of vinegar or lemon juice and use a plant-based butter alternative.

- If you prefer a sweeter bread, increase the honey to 1/3 cup.

- Add 1/2 cup of your favorite nuts or dried fruits, such as walnuts or raisins, to the batter for added texture and flavor.

24. Einkorn Rosemary Focaccia

Number of servings: 8

Preparation time: 20 minutes

Cooking time: 25 minutes

Ingredients:

- 3 cups fresh-milled einkorn flour

- 1 packet (2 1/4 teaspoons) active dry yeast

- 1 teaspoon sugar

- 1 1/2 cups warm water (about 110°F)

- 2 tablespoons olive oil, plus more for drizzling

- 2 teaspoons sea salt, plus more for sprinkling

- 2 tablespoons fresh rosemary, chopped

- 2 cloves garlic, thinly sliced (optional)

Directions:

1. In a large mixing bowl, combine the yeast, sugar, and warm water. Stir gently and let sit for 5 minutes, or until the mixture becomes frothy.

2. Add the fresh-milled einkorn flour, olive oil, and 2 teaspoons of sea salt to the yeast mixture. Stir until a dough forms.

3. Turn the dough out onto a floured surface and knead for about 5 minutes, until smooth and elastic. If the dough is too sticky, add a little more flour as needed.

4. Place the dough in a greased bowl, cover with a clean kitchen towel, and let rise in a warm place for about 1 hour, or until doubled in size.

5. Preheat your oven to 425°F (220°C). Grease a large baking sheet or line it with parchment paper.

6. Punch down the dough and transfer it to the prepared baking sheet. Stretch and press the dough into a roughly 10x15-inch rectangle.

7. Use your fingers to dimple the surface of the dough, then drizzle with additional olive oil. Sprinkle the chopped rosemary, sliced garlic (if using), and a generous pinch of sea salt over the top.

8. Let the dough rest for 10 minutes, then bake in the preheated oven for 20-25 minutes, or until golden brown and crisp.

9. Remove from the oven and let cool slightly before slicing and serving.

Nutritional value per serving:

- Calories: 210

- Carbs: 38g

- Fiber: 4g

- Sugars: 1g

- Protein: 6g

- Saturated fat: 0.5g

- Unsaturated fat: 3g

Difficulty rating: Easy

Tips for ingredient variations:

- For a cheesy version, sprinkle grated Parmesan or Asiago cheese over the focaccia before baking.

- Add sliced olives, sun-dried tomatoes, or caramelized onions on top for additional flavor.

- For a spicier kick, mix red pepper flakes into the dough or sprinkle on top before baking.

25. Einkorn Garlic Herb Breadsticks

Number of servings: 12 breadsticks

Preparation time: 1 hour 15 minutes

Cooking time: 15 minutes

Ingredients:

- 2 1/2 cups fresh-milled einkorn flour
- 1 tablespoon active dry yeast
- 1 teaspoon sugar
- 1 cup warm water (about 110°F)
- 2 tablespoons olive oil
- 2 garlic cloves, minced
- 1 teaspoon salt
- 1 tablespoon dried Italian herbs (such as a mix of oregano, basil, and thyme)
- 1/4 cup unsalted butter, melted
- Coarse sea salt for sprinkling

Directions:

1. In a small bowl, dissolve the yeast and sugar in warm water. Let it sit for 5 minutes until frothy.

2. In a large mixing bowl, combine the fresh-milled einkorn flour, minced garlic, salt, and dried Italian herbs.

3. Add the yeast mixture and olive oil to the flour mixture. Stir until a dough forms.

4. Turn the dough out onto a floured surface and knead for about 5 minutes, until smooth and elastic. Add more flour if the dough is too sticky.

5. Place the dough in a greased bowl, cover with a clean cloth, and let it rise in a warm place for about 1 hour, or until doubled in size.

6. Preheat your oven to 425°F (220°C). Line a baking sheet with parchment paper.

7. Punch down the dough and turn it out onto a floured surface. Divide the dough into 12 equal pieces.

8. Roll each piece into a rope about 8 inches long. Place the ropes on the prepared baking sheet, leaving space between each.

9. Brush the tops of the breadsticks with melted butter and sprinkle with coarse sea salt.

10. Bake in the preheated oven for 15 minutes, or until golden brown.

11. Remove from the oven and let cool slightly on a wire rack before serving.

Nutritional value per serving: (per breadstick)

- Calories: 150
- Carbs: 20g
- Fiber: 1g
- Sugars: 0.5g
- Protein: 3g
- Saturated fat: 2g
- Unsaturated fat: 1g

Difficulty rating: Medium

Tips for ingredient variations:

- For a cheesy version, sprinkle grated Parmesan or Asiago cheese on the breadsticks before baking.

- Add a spicy kick by mixing in 1/2 teaspoon of red pepper flakes into the dough.

- For a garlic butter version, mix additional minced garlic into the melted butter before brushing it on the breadsticks.

26. Einkorn Multigrain Loaf

Number of servings: 1 loaf (12 slices)

Preparation time: 20 minutes

Cooking time: 50 minutes

Ingredients:

- 2 cups fresh-milled einkorn flour
- 1 cup multigrain mix (such as a combination of oats, flaxseed, sunflower seeds, and millet)
- 1 tablespoon baking powder
- 1/2 teaspoon salt
- 1/4 cup honey or maple syrup
- 1 cup buttermilk
- 2 large eggs
- 1/4 cup olive oil
- 1/2 cup walnuts, chopped (optional)

Directions:

1. Preheat your oven to 375°F (190°C). Grease a 9x5 inch loaf pan or line it with parchment paper.

2. In a large mixing bowl, whisk together the fresh-milled einkorn flour, multigrain mix, baking powder, and salt.

3. In a separate bowl, mix the honey (or maple syrup), buttermilk, eggs, and olive oil until well combined.

4. Pour the wet ingredients into the dry ingredients and stir until just combined. Avoid overmixing to prevent the loaf from becoming tough.

5. Fold in the chopped walnuts, if using, until evenly distributed.

6. Pour the batter into the prepared loaf pan and smooth the top with a spatula.

7. Bake in the preheated oven for 50 minutes, or until a toothpick inserted into the center comes out clean.

8. Remove the loaf from the oven and let it cool in the pan for 10 minutes. Then, transfer it to a wire rack to cool completely before slicing.

Nutritional value per serving: (per slice)

- Calories: 210
- Carbs: 28g
- Fiber: 4g
- Sugars: 8g
- Protein: 6g
- Saturated fat: 1g
- Unsaturated fat: 3g

Difficulty rating: Easy

Tips for ingredient variations:

- For a vegan version, substitute the buttermilk with a plant-based milk mixed with 1 tablespoon of vinegar or lemon juice and use maple syrup instead of honey. Replace the eggs with flax eggs (1 flax egg = 1 tablespoon ground flaxseed mixed with 3 tablespoons water, let sit for 15 minutes).

- Feel free to customize the multigrain mix based on your preferences or what you have on hand. Other great additions include pumpkin seeds, sesame seeds, or quinoa.

- If you prefer a sweeter loaf, increase the honey or maple syrup to 1/3 cup and add dried fruits like raisins or cranberries to the batter.

27. Einkorn Olive Bread

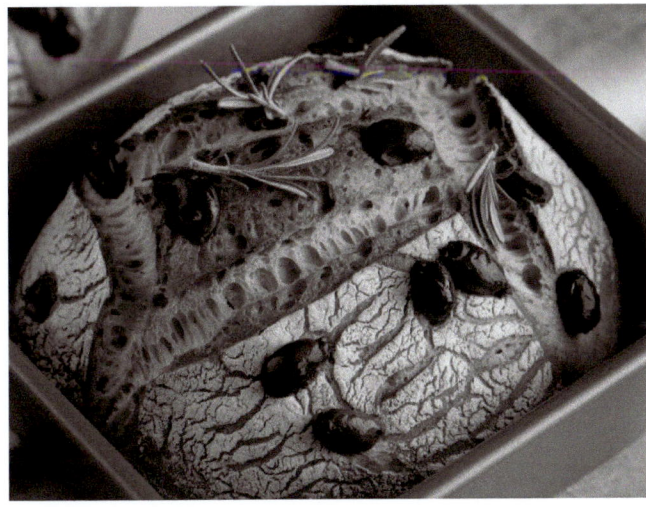

Number of servings: 1 loaf (about 8-10 slices)

Preparation time: 20 minutes

Cooking time: 40 minutes

Ingredients:

- 3 cups fresh-milled einkorn flour
- 1 tablespoon active dry yeast
- 1 teaspoon salt
- 1 tablespoon honey
- 1 1/4 cups warm water (about 110°F)
- 1/4 cup olive oil, plus extra for greasing
- 1 cup pitted and chopped kalamata olives
- 2 tablespoons fresh rosemary, finely chopped

Directions:

1. In a large mixing bowl, combine the fresh-milled einkorn flour, active dry yeast, and salt.

2. In a separate bowl, dissolve the honey in warm water and then add it to the flour mixture along with 1/4 cup olive oil. Stir until a sticky dough forms.

3. Fold in the chopped kalamata olives and fresh rosemary until evenly distributed throughout the dough.

4. Transfer the dough to a lightly floured surface and knead for about 5 minutes, or until it becomes smooth and elastic. Einkorn flour dough will be stickier than traditional wheat dough, so handle with lightly oiled hands if necessary.

5. Place the dough in a greased bowl, cover with a clean kitchen towel, and let it rise in a warm place for about 1 hour, or until doubled in size.

6. Preheat the oven to 375°F (190°C). Gently punch down the risen dough to release any air bubbles.

7. Shape the dough into a loaf and place it in a greased 9x5 inch loaf pan. Let it rise again for about 30 minutes, or until puffy.

8. Bake in the preheated oven for 40 minutes, or until the top is golden brown and the loaf sounds hollow when tapped on the bottom.

9. Remove from the oven and let cool in the pan for 10 minutes, then transfer to a wire rack to cool completely before slicing.

Nutritional value per serving: (based on 10 slices per loaf)

- Calories: 210
- Carbs: 32g
- Fiber: 4g
- Sugars: 1g
- Protein: 5g
- Saturated fat: 1g
- Unsaturated fat: 3g

Difficulty rating: Medium

Tips for ingredient variations:

- For a different flavor profile, substitute the kalamata olives with green olives or a mix of both.

- Add 1/2 cup of grated Parmesan or feta cheese to the dough for a cheesy twist.

- If rosemary is not your herb of choice, try using thyme or oregano for a different taste.

28. Einkorn Pita Bread

Number of servings: 8 pita breads

Preparation time: 1 hour 15 minutes (including resting time)

Cooking time: 6-8 minutes

Ingredients:

- 2 cups fresh-milled einkorn flour
- 1 teaspoon salt
- 1 teaspoon instant yeast
- 1 tablespoon olive oil
- 3/4 cup warm water

Directions:

1. In a large mixing bowl, combine the fresh-milled einkorn flour, salt, and instant yeast.

2. Add the olive oil and warm water to the dry ingredients. Stir with a wooden spoon until a dough forms.

3. Knead the dough on a lightly floured surface for about 5 minutes, until it becomes smooth and elastic. Einkorn dough may feel a bit stickier than dough made with modern wheat flour, so resist the urge to add too much additional flour.

4. Place the dough in a lightly oiled bowl, cover with a clean kitchen towel, and let it rest in a warm place for 1 hour, or until it doubles in size.

5. Preheat your oven to 475°F (245°C) and place a baking stone or inverted baking sheet inside to heat.

6. After the dough has risen, punch it down gently and divide it into 8 equal pieces. Roll each piece into a ball, then flatten into a disk. On a lightly floured surface, roll out each disk into a circle about 1/4 inch thick.

7. Place the rolled-out pitas directly onto the hot baking stone or inverted baking sheet. Bake for 2-3 minutes, until the pitas puff up. Flip and bake for an additional 2-3 minutes, until lightly golden.

8. Remove the pitas from the oven and wrap them in a clean kitchen towel to keep them soft.

Nutritional value per serving:

- Calories: 140
- Carbs: 26g
- Fiber: 4g
- Sugars: 0g
- Protein: 4g
- Saturated fat: 0.5g
- Unsaturated fat: 1g

Difficulty rating: Easy

Tips for ingredient variations:

- For a whole grain version, substitute half of the fresh-milled einkorn flour with fresh-milled einkorn whole grain flour.

- Add herbs such as rosemary or thyme to the dough for a flavorful twist.

- For a garlic pita bread, knead 1 teaspoon of garlic powder into the dough before the first rise.

29. Einkorn Rye Bread

Number of servings: 1 loaf (about 12 slices)

Preparation time: 20 minutes

Cooking time: 50 minutes

Ingredients:

- 2 cups fresh-milled einkorn flour
- 1 cup rye flour
- 1 tablespoon instant yeast
- 1 teaspoon salt
- 1 tablespoon molasses
- 1 1/4 cups warm water
- 2 tablespoons olive oil
- 1 tablespoon caraway seeds (optional)

Directions:

1. In a large mixing bowl, combine the fresh-milled einkorn flour, rye flour, instant yeast, and salt.

2. In a separate bowl, mix the molasses with the warm water until fully dissolved.

3. Add the molasses mixture and olive oil to the dry ingredients. Stir until a sticky dough forms. If using, fold in the caraway seeds at this stage.

4. Transfer the dough to a floured surface and knead for about 10 minutes, or until smooth and elastic. Einkorn flour makes the dough slightly stickier than conventional flour, so avoid adding too much extra flour during kneading.

5. Shape the dough into a loaf and place it in a greased 9x5 inch loaf pan.

6. Cover the pan with a clean kitchen towel and let the dough rise in a warm place for about 1 hour, or until it has doubled in size.

7. Preheat your oven to 375°F (190°C).

8. Bake the risen loaf for 50 minutes, or until the top is golden brown and a toothpick inserted into the center comes out clean.

9. Remove the bread from the oven and let it cool in the pan for 10 minutes. Then, transfer it to a wire rack to cool completely before slicing.

Nutritional value per serving: (per slice, based on 12 slices per loaf)

- Calories: 150
- Carbs: 28g
- Fiber: 4g
- Sugars: 2g
- Protein: 4g
- Saturated fat: 0.5g
- Unsaturated fat: 2g

Difficulty rating: Medium

Tips for ingredient variations:

- For a sweeter loaf, increase the amount of molasses to 2 tablespoons.

- If you're not a fan of caraway seeds, you can omit them or substitute with fennel seeds for a different flavor profile.

- To create a crustier loaf, spray the oven with water just before baking and again halfway through the cooking time.

30. Einkorn Brioche

Number of servings: 8

Preparation time: 2 hours 30 minutes

Cooking time: 35 minutes

Ingredients:

- 3 1/2 cups fresh-milled einkorn flour
- 1/4 cup granulated sugar
- 1/2 teaspoon salt
- 4 large eggs, at room temperature
- 1 tablespoon active dry yeast
- 1/4 cup warm water (about 110°F)
- 1 cup unsalted butter, softened
- 1 egg, beaten (for egg wash)

Directions:

1. In a small bowl, dissolve the yeast in warm water with a pinch of sugar. Let it sit until frothy, about 5-10 minutes.

2. In a large mixing bowl, combine the fresh-milled einkorn flour, sugar, and salt.

3. Add the eggs to the flour mixture, one at a time, mixing well after each addition.

4. Add the yeast mixture to the bowl and mix until a dough starts to form.

5. Gradually add the softened butter, a few tablespoons at a time, kneading well after each addition. The dough will be very soft and sticky.

6. Transfer the dough to a lightly floured surface and knead for about 10 minutes, until smooth and elastic. Add a little more flour if necessary, but keep it to a minimum to ensure a tender brioche.

7. Place the dough in a greased bowl, cover with a clean kitchen towel, and let it rise in a warm place until doubled in size, about 1-1.5 hours.

8. Punch down the dough, then divide it into 8 equal pieces. Shape each piece into a ball and place them in a greased 9x13 inch baking pan.

9. Cover the pan with a towel and let the dough rise again until puffy, about 1 hour.

10. Preheat the oven to 375°F (190°C).

11. Brush the top of the brioche with beaten egg for a glossy finish.

12. Bake for 35 minutes, or until the brioche is golden brown and sounds hollow when tapped on the bottom.

13. Remove from the oven and let cool on a wire rack before serving.

Nutritional value per serving: Calories: 450, Carbs: 45g, Fiber: 2g, Sugars: 6g, Protein: 9g, Saturated fat: 15g, Unsaturated fat: 5g

Difficulty rating: Medium

Tips for ingredient variations:

- For a sweeter brioche, increase the sugar to 1/3 cup and add 1 teaspoon of vanilla extract to the dough.

- Incorporate 1/2 cup of chocolate chips or dried fruit such as raisins or cranberries into the dough before the second rise for a flavorful twist.

- For a savory version, reduce the sugar to 1 tablespoon and add 1/2 cup of grated cheese and 1/4 cup of finely chopped herbs to the dough.

31. Einkorn Flatbread

Number of servings: 6

Preparation time: 15 minutes

Cooking time: 10 minutes

Ingredients:

- 2 cups fresh-milled einkorn flour
- 1 teaspoon salt
- 1/2 teaspoon baking powder
- 2 tablespoons olive oil
- 3/4 cup warm water

Directions:

1. In a large mixing bowl, combine the fresh-milled einkorn flour, salt, and baking powder.

2. Add the olive oil and gradually mix in the warm water until a dough forms. You may need slightly more or less water, so add it gradually until the dough is soft and pliable but not sticky.

3. Turn the dough out onto a floured surface and knead for about 5 minutes, until it becomes smooth and elastic.

4. Divide the dough into 6 equal portions. Roll each portion into a ball, then flatten and roll out into a circle about 1/8 inch thick.

5. Heat a large skillet or griddle over medium-high heat. Once hot, place one flatbread in the skillet and cook for about 1-2 minutes on each side, or until the flatbread puffs up and has golden brown spots. No oil is needed if using a non-stick pan.

6. Remove the cooked flatbread and wrap it in a clean kitchen towel to keep warm. Repeat with the remaining dough.

7. Serve the einkorn flatbreads warm as a side dish or use them as a base for your favorite toppings.

Nutritional value per serving:

- Calories: 200
- Carbs: 32g
- Fiber: 4g
- Sugars: 0g
- Protein: 5g
- Saturated fat: 1g
- Unsaturated fat: 2g

Difficulty rating: Easy

Tips for ingredient variations:

- For a herbed flatbread, add 1 teaspoon of dried herbs such as rosemary or thyme to the flour mixture.

- For a garlic flatbread, add 1 minced garlic clove to the dough or brush the cooked flatbreads with garlic-infused olive oil.

- To make the flatbread richer, substitute the water with milk and add an extra tablespoon of olive oil.

32. Einkorn Pull-Apart Rolls

Number of servings: 12 rolls

Preparation time: 2 hours 30 minutes

Cooking time: 20 minutes

Ingredients:

- 3 1/2 cups fresh-milled einkorn flour
- 1 cup warm water (about 110°F)
- 1/4 cup honey
- 2 1/4 teaspoons active dry yeast (1 packet)
- 1/4 cup unsalted butter, melted
- 1 teaspoon salt
- 1/2 teaspoon garlic powder (optional for flavor)
- 1/4 cup fresh herbs (such as rosemary and thyme), finely chopped (optional for flavor)
- Olive oil for greasing the bowl and pan
- 1 egg, beaten (for egg wash)

Directions:

1. In a large mixing bowl, dissolve the honey in warm water. Sprinkle the yeast over the water and let it sit for 5-10 minutes until frothy.

2. Add 2 cups of einkorn flour, melted butter, salt, garlic powder, and herbs (if using) to the yeast mixture. Stir until well combined.

3. Gradually add the remaining einkorn flour, 1/2 cup at a time, until a soft dough forms. You may not need all the flour, as einkorn dough can be stickier than traditional wheat dough.

4. Transfer the dough to a floured surface and knead for about 5 minutes, until smooth and elastic. Add a little more flour if the dough is too sticky to handle, but try to keep it as hydrated as possible.

5. Place the dough in a greased bowl, turning once to coat. Cover with a clean kitchen towel and let it rise in a warm place for about 1 hour, or until doubled in size.

6. Punch down the dough and turn it out onto a lightly floured surface. Divide the dough into 12 equal pieces and shape each piece into a ball.

7. Arrange the dough balls in a greased 9x13 inch baking pan, leaving some space between each for them to expand. Cover and let rise for another 30 minutes, or until nearly doubled.

8. Preheat your oven to 375°F (190°C).

9. Gently brush the tops of the rolls with beaten egg to give them a shiny, golden finish.

10. Bake in the preheated oven for 20 minutes, or until the rolls are golden brown and sound hollow when tapped on the bottom.

11. Remove from the oven and let cool for a few minutes before serving.

Nutritional value per serving: (per roll)

- Calories: 180
- Carbs: 30g
- Fiber: 4g
- Sugars: 5g
- Protein: 5g
- Saturated fat: 2g
- Unsaturated fat: 1g

Difficulty rating: Medium

Tips for ingredient variations:

- For a sweeter roll, increase the honey to 1/3 cup and omit the garlic powder and herbs.

- Add 1/2 cup of grated cheese such as Parmesan or cheddar to the dough for cheesy rolls.

- For a whole grain variation, substitute 1 cup of the einkorn flour with fresh-milled einkorn whole grain flour. Adjust the water as needed, as whole grain flour may absorb more liquid.

33. Einkorn Pumpkin Bread

Number of servings: 1 loaf (10 slices)

Preparation time: 15 minutes

Cooking time: 60 minutes

Ingredients:

- 2 cups fresh-milled einkorn flour
- 1 teaspoon baking soda
- 1/2 teaspoon salt
- 1 teaspoon ground cinnamon
- 1/4 teaspoon ground nutmeg
- 1/4 teaspoon ground cloves
- 1/4 cup unsalted butter, melted
- 1/2 cup brown sugar
- 1/4 cup granulated sugar
- 2 large eggs
- 1 cup pumpkin puree
- 1/4 cup water
- 1 teaspoon vanilla extract
- 1/2 cup walnuts, chopped (optional)

Directions:

1. Preheat your oven to 350°F (175°C). Grease and flour a 9x5 inch loaf pan.

2. In a medium bowl, whisk together the fresh-milled einkorn flour, baking soda, salt, cinnamon, nutmeg, and cloves. Set aside.

3. In a large bowl, mix the melted butter, brown sugar, and granulated sugar until well combined. Beat in the eggs, one at a time, then stir in the pumpkin puree, water, and vanilla extract.

4. Gradually add the dry ingredients to the pumpkin mixture, stirring until just combined. Fold in the walnuts, if using.

5. Pour the batter into the prepared loaf pan. Smooth the top with a spatula.

6. Bake for 60 minutes, or until a toothpick inserted into the center of the loaf comes out clean.

7. Let the bread cool in the pan for 10 minutes, then turn out onto a wire rack to cool completely.

Nutritional value per serving: (1 slice)

- Calories: 210
- Carbs: 30g
- Fiber: 2g
- Sugars: 15g
- Protein: 4g
- Saturated fat: 3g
- Unsaturated fat: 2g

Difficulty rating: Easy

Tips for ingredient variations:

- Substitute walnuts with pecans or leave them out for a nut-free version.

- Add 1/2 cup of chocolate chips or dried cranberries for a sweeter, fruitier loaf.

- For a dairy-free version, use coconut oil instead of butter.

34. Einkorn Challah

Number of servings: 2 loaves

Preparation time: 3 hours

Cooking time: 35 minutes

Ingredients:

- 4 cups fresh-milled einkorn flour
- 1/2 cup warm water
- 2 teaspoons active dry yeast
- 1/4 cup honey
- 2 large eggs, plus 1 for glazing
- 1/4 cup olive oil
- 1 teaspoon salt
- Sesame or poppy seeds for topping (optional)

Directions:

1. In a small bowl, dissolve the yeast in the warm water and let it sit until frothy, about 5 minutes.

2. In a large mixing bowl, combine the fresh-milled einkorn flour and salt.

3. Make a well in the center of the flour mixture and add the yeast mixture, honey, 2 eggs, and olive oil.

4. Mix until a dough forms, then knead on a lightly floured surface for about 10 minutes, until the dough is smooth and elastic.

5. Place the dough in a greased bowl, cover with a clean cloth, and let it rise in a warm place for about 1.5 hours, or until doubled in size.

6. Punch down the dough and divide it into six equal pieces. Roll each piece into a long strand, about 12 inches long.

7. Take three strands and pinch them together at one end. Braid the strands, then pinch the ends together and tuck them under. Repeat with the remaining three strands to form the second loaf.

8. Place the braided loaves on a baking sheet lined with parchment paper, cover them with a cloth, and let them rise again for about 1 hour, or until puffed up.

9. Preheat your oven to 375°F (190°C).

10. Beat the remaining egg and brush it over the top of the loaves. Sprinkle with sesame or poppy seeds if desired.

11. Bake in the preheated oven for 35 minutes, or until the loaves are golden brown and sound hollow when tapped on the bottom.

12. Remove from the oven and let cool on a wire rack before slicing.

Nutritional value per serving: (per slice, based on 16 slices per loaf)

- Calories: 140
- Carbs: 23g
- Fiber: 1g
- Sugars: 3g
- Protein: 4g
- Saturated fat: 0.5g
- Unsaturated fat: 2g

Difficulty rating: Medium

Tips for ingredient variations:

- For a sweeter challah, increase the honey to 1/3 cup and add 1/2 cup of raisins to the dough before the first rise.

- Substitute olive oil with melted butter for a richer flavor.

- Add 1 teaspoon of cinnamon to the dough for a spiced challah.

35. Einkorn Ciabatta

Number of servings: 1 large loaf

Preparation time: 2 hours 20 minutes (including rise time)

Cooking time: 25 minutes

Ingredients:

- 3 cups fresh-milled einkorn flour
- 1 1/4 teaspoons salt
- 1/4 teaspoon active dry yeast
- 1 1/3 cups warm water
- Cornmeal or flour, for dusting

Directions:

1. In a large bowl, combine the einkorn flour, salt, and yeast. Add the warm water, and stir until a shaggy dough forms.

2. Cover the bowl with a clean kitchen towel and let it sit at room temperature for about 2 hours, until the dough has doubled in size and is bubbly on the surface.

3. After the first rise, gently fold the dough over onto itself a couple of times on a lightly floured surface. Shape the dough into a rough ball.

4. Place a piece of parchment paper on your work surface and generously dust it with cornmeal or flour. Transfer the dough ball onto the parchment paper, seam side down. Cover it loosely with the kitchen towel and let it rise for another 30 minutes.

5. Preheat your oven to 450°F (232°C). Place a Dutch oven with its lid in the oven as it preheats.

6. After the second rise, carefully remove the hot Dutch oven from the oven. Lift the dough using the parchment paper and lower it into the Dutch oven. Cover with the lid.

7. Bake in the preheated oven for 20 minutes. After 20 minutes, remove the lid and bake for an additional 5 minutes, or until the crust is golden brown and crispy.

8. Carefully remove the bread from the Dutch oven and let it cool on a wire rack for at least 1 hour before slicing.

Nutritional value per serving: (Based on 8 servings per loaf)

- Calories: 160
- Carbs: 34g
- Fiber: 1g
- Sugars: 0g
- Protein: 4g
- Saturated fat: 0g
- Unsaturated fat: 0g

Difficulty rating: Medium

Tips for ingredient variations:

- For a more rustic flavor, mix in 1/2 cup of whole fresh-milled einkorn grains with the flour.

- Add 1 tablespoon of dried herbs like rosemary or thyme to the dough for an aromatic twist.

- Incorporate 1/2 cup of olives or sun-dried tomatoes into the dough after the first rise for a Mediterranean-inspired ciabatta.

36. Einkorn Pretzel Rolls

Number of servings: 8 rolls

Preparation time: 2 hours 30 minutes

Cooking time: 15 minutes

Ingredients:

- 1 1/2 cups warm water (110°F)

- 1 tablespoon sugar

- 2 teaspoons active dry yeast

- 4 1/2 cups fresh-milled einkorn flour, plus more for dusting

- 2 teaspoons salt

- 4 tablespoons unsalted butter, melted

- 10 cups water

- 2/3 cup baking soda

- Coarse sea salt, for sprinkling

Directions:

1. In a small bowl, dissolve the sugar in warm water and sprinkle the yeast over the top. Let it sit for 5-10 minutes, or until the mixture is frothy.

2. In a large mixing bowl, combine the fresh-milled einkorn flour and salt. Add the melted butter and yeast mixture, stirring until a dough forms.

3. Turn the dough out onto a lightly floured surface and knead for about 8-10 minutes, until smooth and elastic. Add more flour if the dough is too sticky.

4. Place the dough in a greased bowl, cover with a damp cloth, and let it rise in a warm place for about 1 hour, or until doubled in size.

5. Preheat your oven to 450°F (232°C). Line two baking sheets with parchment paper and lightly grease them.

6. Bring the 10 cups of water to a boil in a large pot. Gradually add the baking soda.

7. Divide the risen dough into 8 equal pieces. Roll each piece into a long rope, then form into a pretzel shape.

8. One at a time, gently drop the pretzels into the boiling water for 30 seconds, removing them with a slotted spoon and placing them on the prepared baking sheets.

9. Sprinkle the boiled pretzels with coarse sea salt while they are still wet.

10. Bake in the preheated oven for 12-15 minutes, or until golden brown.

11. Remove from the oven and let cool on a wire rack for at least 5 minutes before serving.

Nutritional value per serving: Calories: 280, Carbs: 48g, Fiber: 6g, Sugars: 2g, Protein: 8g, Saturated fat: 3g, Unsaturated fat: 1g

Difficulty rating: Medium

Tips for ingredient variations:

- For a sweeter version, brush the pretzels with melted butter and sprinkle with cinnamon sugar after boiling.

- Add minced garlic or garlic powder to the dough for a garlic-flavored pretzel.

- For a cheesy pretzel, sprinkle grated Parmesan or cheddar cheese over the pretzels before baking.

37. Einkorn Naan

Number of servings: 6

Preparation time: 1 hour 15 minutes (includes resting time)

Cooking time: 10 minutes

Ingredients:

- 2 cups fresh-milled einkorn flour, plus extra for dusting
- 1/2 teaspoon salt
- 1/2 teaspoon baking powder
- 3/4 cup lukewarm water
- 2 tablespoons olive oil, plus extra for cooking

Directions:

1. In a large mixing bowl, whisk together the einkorn flour, salt, and baking powder.

2. Make a well in the center of the flour mixture and add the lukewarm water and olive oil.

3. Gradually mix the flour into the water and oil, using your hands or a wooden spoon, until a soft dough forms.

4. Turn the dough out onto a lightly floured surface and knead for about 5 minutes, until it is smooth and elastic. Add a little more flour if the dough is too sticky.

5. Place the dough back in the bowl, cover with a clean kitchen towel, and let it rest for 1 hour at room temperature.

6. After resting, divide the dough into 6 equal portions. Roll each portion into a ball.

7. On a lightly floured surface, roll out each ball into a thin circle, about 1/8 inch thick.

8. Heat a large skillet or griddle over medium-high heat and brush lightly with olive oil.

9. Cook each naan for about 1-2 minutes on each side, or until puffed up and golden brown spots appear. Brush the skillet with additional olive oil as needed between naans.

10. Serve the naan warm.

Nutritional value per serving: (per naan)

- Calories: 180
- Carbs: 30g
- Fiber: 4g
- Sugars: 0g
- Protein: 5g
- Saturated fat: 0.5g
- Unsaturated fat: 2g

Difficulty rating: Easy

Tips for ingredient variations:

- For a garlic naan, finely mince 2 cloves of garlic and brush over the naan with olive oil before cooking.

- Add fresh herbs such as chopped cilantro or parsley to the dough for an aromatic twist.

- For a richer flavor, substitute the water with whole milk or yogurt, adjusting the quantity as needed to form a soft dough.

38. Einkorn Country Loaf

Number of servings: 1 loaf (about 12 slices)

Preparation time: 15 minutes

Cooking time: 40 minutes

Ingredients:

- 3 cups fresh-milled einkorn flour

- 1 1/4 cups warm water (about 110°F)

- 2 teaspoons instant yeast

- 1 teaspoon salt

- 1 tablespoon honey

- 1 tablespoon olive oil (plus extra for greasing the bowl and pan)

Directions:

1. In a large mixing bowl, combine the warm water, instant yeast, and honey. Stir gently and let sit for 5 minutes, or until the mixture becomes frothy, indicating that the yeast is active.

2. Add the fresh-milled einkorn flour and salt to the yeast mixture. Mix until a shaggy dough forms.

3. Drizzle the olive oil over the dough, then knead in the bowl for about 5 minutes. The dough should be slightly sticky but manageable. If it's too sticky, add a bit more flour, one tablespoon at a time.

4. Transfer the dough to a lightly oiled bowl, turning it to coat all sides with oil. Cover the bowl with a clean kitchen towel and let it rise in a warm, draft-free place for about 1 hour, or until doubled in size.

5. Preheat your oven to 375°F (190°C). Gently punch down the risen dough to release any air bubbles.

6. Shape the dough into a loaf and place it in a lightly oiled 9x5 inch loaf pan. Cover loosely with the kitchen towel and let it rise again for about 30 minutes, or until it puffs up slightly above the rim of the pan.

7. Bake in the preheated oven for 40 minutes, or until the top is golden brown and the loaf sounds hollow when tapped on the bottom.

8. Remove the loaf from the oven and let it cool in the pan for 10 minutes. Then, transfer it to a wire rack to cool completely before slicing.

Nutritional value per serving: (per slice, based on 12 slices per loaf)

- Calories: 150

- Carbs: 28g

- Fiber: 4g

- Sugars: 1g

- Protein: 5g

- Saturated fat: 0.5g

- Unsaturated fat: 1g

Difficulty rating: Medium

Tips for ingredient variations:

- For a sweeter loaf, increase the honey to 2 tablespoons.

- Add 1/2 cup of mix-ins like chopped olives, sun-dried tomatoes, or nuts for added texture and flavor.

- For a whole grain version, substitute 1 cup of the einkorn flour with fresh-milled einkorn whole grain flour.

- Brush the top of the loaf with a mixture of water and honey before baking for a shiny, golden crust.

39. Einkorn Seeded Bread

Number of servings: 1 loaf (about 12 slices)

Preparation time: 20 minutes

Cooking time: 50 minutes

Ingredients:

- 3 cups fresh-milled einkorn flour
- 1 tablespoon active dry yeast
- 1 teaspoon salt
- 1 tablespoon honey
- 1 1/4 cups warm water (about 110°F)
- 2 tablespoons olive oil
- 1/2 cup mixed seeds (sunflower seeds, pumpkin seeds, flaxseeds, sesame seeds)
- Additional seeds for topping

Directions:

1. In a large mixing bowl, combine the fresh-milled einkorn flour, active dry yeast, and salt.

2. In a separate bowl, dissolve the honey in warm water, then add the olive oil.

3. Gradually add the wet ingredients to the dry ingredients, stirring until a dough begins to form.

4. Fold in the mixed seeds until evenly distributed throughout the dough.

5. Transfer the dough to a floured surface and knead for about 10 minutes, until smooth and elastic.

6. Place the dough in a greased bowl, cover with a damp cloth, and let it rise in a warm place for about 1 hour, or until doubled in size.

7. Punch down the dough and shape it into a loaf. Place the loaf in a greased 9x5 inch loaf pan. Sprinkle the top with additional seeds.

8. Cover and let rise again for about 30 minutes, or until the dough has risen about 1 inch above the pan.

9. Preheat the oven to 375°F (190°C).

10. Bake the loaf for about 50 minutes, or until the bread is golden brown and sounds hollow when tapped on the bottom.

11. Remove from the oven and let cool in the pan for 10 minutes, then transfer to a wire rack to cool completely before slicing.

Nutritional value per serving: (per slice, based on 12 slices per loaf)

- Calories: 180
- Carbs: 28g
- Fiber: 4g
- Sugars: 1g
- Protein: 6g
- Saturated fat: 0.5g
- Unsaturated fat: 2g

Difficulty rating: Medium

Tips for ingredient variations:

- For a nuttier flavor, add 1/4 cup of chopped walnuts or almonds to the dough.

- If you prefer a sweeter bread, increase the honey to 2 tablespoons.

- For a different seed mix, try using chia seeds or poppy seeds in place of or in addition to the suggested seeds.

40. Einkorn Baguette

Number of servings: 2 baguettes

Preparation time: 2 hours 30 minutes

Cooking time: 25 minutes

Ingredients:

- 4 cups fresh-milled einkorn flour
- 1 1/2 teaspoons salt
- 1 teaspoon instant yeast
- 1 3/4 cups lukewarm water

Directions:

1. In a large mixing bowl, whisk together the einkorn flour, salt, and instant yeast.

2. Add the lukewarm water to the dry ingredients, and stir with a wooden spoon until a shaggy dough forms.

3. Cover the bowl with a clean kitchen towel and let the dough rest at room temperature for 2 hours, or until it has doubled in size.

4. Gently turn the dough out onto a lightly floured surface. Divide the dough in half.

5. Shape each half into a long, thin loaf, about 14 inches in length, by rolling and stretching the dough gently with your hands.

6. Place the shaped loaves onto a baking sheet lined with parchment paper, making sure they are several inches apart.

7. Cover the loaves with a lightly greased piece of plastic wrap and let them rise for an additional 30 minutes, or until they have puffed up slightly.

8. Preheat your oven to 450°F (232°C). Place a shallow metal or cast-iron pan on the bottom rack of the oven.

9. Right before baking, slash the tops of the loaves 3 or 4 times diagonally using a sharp knife.

10. Place the baking sheet on the middle rack of the oven. Pour 1 cup of hot water into the preheated pan on the bottom rack to create steam.

11. Bake the baguettes for 25 minutes, or until they are golden brown and sound hollow when tapped on the bottom.

12. Remove the baguettes from the oven and let them cool on a wire rack for at least 20 minutes before slicing.

Nutritional value per serving: (per baguette)

- Calories: 920
- Carbs: 192g
- Fiber: 12g
- Sugars: 1g
- Protein: 32g
- Saturated fat: 0g
- Unsaturated fat: 2g

Difficulty rating: Medium

Tips for ingredient variations:

- For a whole grain version, substitute 1 cup of the einkorn flour with fresh-milled einkorn whole grain flour.

- Add 1 tablespoon of dried herbs, such as rosemary or thyme, to the flour mixture for an herbed baguette.

- For a garlic-infused baguette, add 1 teaspoon of garlic powder to the dough, or brush the loaves with garlic-infused olive oil before baking.

Chapter 4: 20 Dessert Recipes

41. Einkorn Chocolate Chip Cookies

Number of servings: 24 cookies

Preparation time: 15 minutes

Cooking time: 10 minutes

Ingredients:

- 2 1/4 cups fresh-milled einkorn flour
- 1/2 teaspoon baking soda
- 1/2 teaspoon salt
- 3/4 cup unsalted butter, melted
- 1 cup packed brown sugar
- 1/2 cup granulated sugar
- 1 tablespoon vanilla extract
- 1 egg
- 1 egg yolk
- 2 cups semisweet chocolate chips

Directions:

1. Preheat your oven to 325°F (165°C) and line cookie sheets with parchment paper.

2. In a small bowl, sift together the fresh-milled einkorn flour, baking soda, and salt. Set aside.

3. In a large bowl, mix the melted butter, brown sugar, and granulated sugar until well blended.

4. Beat in the vanilla, egg, and egg yolk until light and creamy.

5. Gradually blend in the dry ingredients until just mixed.

6. Stir in the chocolate chips by hand using a wooden spoon.

7. Drop cookie dough 1/4 cup at a time onto the prepared cookie sheets. Cookies should be about 3 inches apart.

8. Bake for 10-12 minutes in the preheated oven, or until the edges are lightly toasted.

9. Cool on baking sheets for a few minutes before transferring to wire racks to cool completely.

Nutritional value per serving:

- Calories: 280
- Carbs: 35g
- Fiber: 2g
- Sugars: 23g
- Protein: 3g
- Saturated fat: 8g
- Unsaturated fat: 3g

Difficulty rating: Easy

Tips for ingredient variations:

- For a healthier twist, substitute half of the chocolate chips with nuts like walnuts or pecans.

- If you prefer a less sweet cookie, reduce the granulated sugar to 1/4 cup.

- For a dairy-free version, use plant-based butter and dairy-free chocolate chips.

42. Einkorn Lemon Bars

Number of servings: 16 bars

Preparation time: 20 minutes

Cooking time: 45 minutes

Ingredients:

For the crust:

- 1 1/2 cups fresh-milled einkorn flour
- 1/4 cup granulated sugar
- 1/2 cup unsalted butter, cold and cubed
- 1/4 teaspoon salt

For the filling:

- 4 large eggs
- 1 1/2 cups granulated sugar
- 3/4 cup fresh lemon juice (about 3-4 lemons)
- 1/4 cup fresh-milled einkorn flour
- Zest of 2 lemons
- Powdered sugar for dusting (optional)

Directions:

1. Preheat your oven to 350°F (175°C). Line a 9x13 inch baking pan with parchment paper, leaving an overhang on the sides for easy removal.

2. Start with the crust by combining 1 1/2 cups einkorn flour, 1/4 cup granulated sugar, and 1/4 teaspoon salt in a mixing bowl. Add the cold, cubed butter and mix using a pastry cutter or your hands until the mixture resembles coarse crumbs.

3. Press the crust mixture evenly into the bottom of the prepared pan. Bake for 18-20 minutes, or until lightly golden. Remove from the oven and let cool slightly while you prepare the filling.

4. For the filling, whisk together the eggs and 1 1/2 cups granulated sugar until well combined. Stir in the lemon juice, then gently fold in 1/4 cup einkorn flour and lemon zest until the mixture is smooth.

5. Pour the filling over the baked crust and return to the oven. Bake for an additional 25-30 minutes, or until the filling is set and no longer wobbles when the pan is shaken.

6. Let the lemon bars cool completely in the pan set on a wire rack. Once cooled, use the parchment paper overhang to lift the bars out of the pan. Cut into squares and dust with powdered sugar before serving, if desired.

Nutritional value per serving: Calories: 220, Carbs: 35g, Fiber: 1g, Sugars: 25g, Protein: 3g, Saturated fat: 5g, Unsaturated fat: 1g

Difficulty rating: Medium

Tips for ingredient variations:

- For a gluten-free version, substitute the einkorn flour with your favorite gluten-free flour blend. Adjust the amount of flour as needed to achieve the right consistency for the crust and filling.

- Add a tablespoon of poppy seeds to the lemon filling for a crunchy texture and additional flavor.

- For a lime twist, replace the lemon juice and zest with lime juice and zest.

43. Einkorn Brownies

Number of servings: 16 brownies

Preparation time: 15 minutes

Cooking time: 25 minutes

Ingredients:

- 1 cup fresh-milled einkorn flour
- 1/2 cup unsweetened cocoa powder
- 1/2 teaspoon salt
- 1/4 teaspoon baking powder
- 2 large eggs
- 1 cup granulated sugar
- 1/2 cup unsalted butter, melted
- 1 teaspoon vanilla extract
- 1/2 cup semi-sweet chocolate chips

Directions:

1. Preheat your oven to 350°F (175°C). Grease an 8x8 inch baking pan or line it with parchment paper.
2. In a medium bowl, whisk together the fresh-milled einkorn flour, cocoa powder, salt, and baking powder. Set aside.
3. In a large bowl, beat the eggs and granulated sugar together until light and fluffy.
4. Stir in the melted butter and vanilla extract until well combined.
5. Gradually add the dry ingredients to the wet ingredients, mixing until just combined. Avoid overmixing.
6. Fold in the semi-sweet chocolate chips.
7. Pour the batter into the prepared baking pan, spreading it evenly with a spatula.
8. Bake in the preheated oven for 25 minutes, or until a toothpick inserted into the center comes out with a few moist crumbs.
9. Allow the brownies to cool in the pan for at least 10 minutes before cutting into squares.

Nutritional value per serving:

- Calories: 200
- Carbs: 27g
- Fiber: 2g
- Sugars: 18g
- Protein: 3g
- Saturated fat: 7g
- Unsaturated fat: 2g

Difficulty rating: Easy

Tips for ingredient variations:

- For a nutty flavor, add 1/2 cup of chopped walnuts or pecans to the batter.
- Substitute the semi-sweet chocolate chips with dark chocolate chips for a richer chocolate taste.
- For a dairy-free version, use coconut oil instead of butter and choose dairy-free chocolate chips.

44. Einkorn Carrot Cake

Number of servings: 12

Preparation time: 30 minutes

Cooking time: 50 minutes

Ingredients:

- 2 cups fresh-milled einkorn flour
- 2 teaspoons baking powder
- 1/2 teaspoon baking soda
- 1/4 teaspoon salt
- 2 teaspoons ground cinnamon
- 1/2 teaspoon ground nutmeg
- 1/4 teaspoon ground ginger
- 4 large eggs
- 1 1/4 cups granulated sugar
- 1 cup vegetable oil
- 2 cups grated carrots
- 1/2 cup crushed pineapple, drained
- 1/2 cup chopped walnuts
- 1/2 cup unsweetened shredded coconut

For the frosting:

- 8 ounces cream cheese, softened
- 1/2 cup unsalted butter, softened
- 4 cups powdered sugar
- 2 teaspoons vanilla extract

Directions:

1. Preheat your oven to 350°F (175°C). Grease and flour a 9x13 inch baking pan.

2. In a medium bowl, whisk together the fresh-milled einkorn flour, baking powder, baking soda, salt, cinnamon, nutmeg, and ginger.

3. In a large bowl, beat the eggs, granulated sugar, and vegetable oil together until smooth.

4. Gradually add the dry ingredients to the wet ingredients, mixing until just combined.

5. Fold in the grated carrots, crushed pineapple, chopped walnuts, and shredded coconut.

6. Pour the batter into the prepared baking pan and smooth the top with a spatula.

7. Bake for 50 minutes, or until a toothpick inserted into the center comes out clean.

8. Allow the cake to cool completely in the pan on a wire rack.

For the frosting:

9. In a large bowl, beat the cream cheese and butter together until smooth.

10. Gradually add the powdered sugar and vanilla extract, beating until the frosting is smooth and spreadable.

11. Spread the frosting evenly over the cooled cake.

Nutritional value per serving: Calories: 650, Carbs: 82g, Fiber: 2g, Sugars: 68g, Protein: 6g, Saturated fat: 15g, Unsaturated fat: 20g

Difficulty rating: Medium

Tips for ingredient variations:

- For a gluten-free version, substitute the einkorn flour with your favorite gluten-free flour blend. Adjust the amount of liquid as needed, as gluten-free flours may absorb moisture differently.

- Replace the vegetable oil with coconut oil for a slightly different flavor profile.

- Add 1/2 cup of raisins or dried cranberries to the batter for extra sweetness and texture.

- For a nut-free cake, omit the walnuts and add an additional 1/4 cup of shredded coconut or crushed pineapple.

45. Einkorn Apple Pie

Number of servings: 8

Preparation time: 1 hour

Cooking time: 45 minutes

Ingredients:

- For the crust:
  - 2 cups fresh-milled einkorn flour
  - 1/2 teaspoon salt
  - 2/3 cup unsalted butter, chilled and cubed
  - 4-6 tablespoons ice water
- For the filling:
  - 6 cups thinly sliced, peeled apples (about 6 medium apples, a mix of Granny Smith and Honeycrisp recommended)
  - 3/4 cup granulated sugar
  - 2 tablespoons fresh-milled einkorn flour
  - 1/2 teaspoon ground cinnamon
  - 1/4 teaspoon ground nutmeg
  - 1 tablespoon lemon juice
  - 1 tablespoon unsalted butter, cut into small pieces

Directions:

1. In a large bowl, combine 2 cups of einkorn flour and 1/2 teaspoon of salt. Cut in 2/3 cup of butter using a pastry blender or two knives until the mixture resembles coarse crumbs.
2. Gradually add ice water, 1 tablespoon at a time, tossing with a fork until the dough holds together when pressed.
3. Shape the dough into a disk, wrap in plastic wrap, and refrigerate for at least 30 minutes.
4. Preheat the oven to 425°F (220°C).
5. On a lightly floured surface, roll out the dough into a 12-inch circle. Transfer to a 9-inch pie plate. Trim the edge, leaving a 1/2-inch overhang.
6. In a large bowl, mix the sliced apples, 3/4 cup of sugar, 2 tablespoons of einkorn flour, cinnamon, nutmeg, and lemon juice. Toss to coat.
7. Spoon the apple mixture into the crust and dot with 1 tablespoon of butter.
8. Roll out the remaining dough for the top crust. Place over the filling. Trim, seal, and flute the edge. Cut slits in the top crust.
9. Bake for 45 minutes or until the crust is golden brown and the filling is bubbly. If necessary, cover the edge of the pie with foil to prevent overbrowning.
10. Remove from the oven and cool on a wire rack before serving.

Nutritional value per serving: Calories: 380, Carbs: 58g, Fiber: 4g, Sugars: 30g, Protein: 4g, Saturated fat: 10g, Unsaturated fat: 3g

Difficulty rating: Medium

Tips for ingredient variations:

- For a healthier filling, reduce the sugar to 1/2 cup and add 1/4 cup of pure maple syrup.
- Mix in 1/2 cup of fresh cranberries with the apples for a tart twist.
- For a crumble topping, mix 1/2 cup of rolled oats, 1/3 cup of brown sugar, 1/4 cup of einkorn flour, and 1/4 cup of softened butter, then sprinkle over the apple mixture before baking.

46. Einkorn Chocolate Cake

Number of servings: 12

Preparation time: 20 minutes

Cooking time: 35 minutes

Ingredients:

- 2 cups fresh-milled einkorn flour
- 3/4 cup unsweetened cocoa powder
- 1 1/2 teaspoons baking soda
- 1/2 teaspoon salt
- 1 cup granulated sugar
- 1/2 cup unsalted butter, softened
- 2 large eggs
- 1 teaspoon vanilla extract
- 1 cup buttermilk
- 1/2 cup boiling water

Directions:

1. Preheat your oven to 350°F (175°C). Grease and flour a 9x13 inch baking pan.

2. In a medium bowl, whisk together the einkorn flour, cocoa powder, baking soda, and salt. Set aside.

3. In a large bowl, beat the sugar and butter together until light and fluffy. Add the eggs, one at a time, beating well after each addition. Stir in the vanilla extract.

4. Gradually add the flour mixture to the butter mixture, alternating with the buttermilk, beginning and ending with the flour mixture. Beat until just combined.

5. Stir in the boiling water until the batter is smooth. The batter will be thin.

6. Pour the batter into the prepared baking pan.

7. Bake for 35 minutes, or until a toothpick inserted into the center comes out clean.

8. Allow the cake to cool in the pan on a wire rack before cutting into squares and serving.

Nutritional value per serving: Calories: 250, Carbs: 38g, Fiber: 2g, Sugars: 22g, Protein: 4g, Saturated fat: 7g, Unsaturated fat: 3g

Difficulty rating: Easy

Tips for ingredient variations:

- For a dairy-free version, substitute the buttermilk with almond milk mixed with 1 tablespoon of vinegar and use a plant-based butter.

- Add 1 cup of chopped nuts or chocolate chips to the batter for added texture.

- For a coffee-flavored cake, replace the boiling water with hot brewed coffee.

47. Einkorn Cheesecake

Number of servings: 8

Preparation time: 30 minutes

Cooking time: 55 minutes

Ingredients:

- For the crust:
  - 1 1/2 cups fresh-milled einkorn flour
  - 1/4 cup granulated sugar
  - 1/2 cup unsalted butter, chilled and cubed
  - 1/4 teaspoon salt
  - 2-3 tablespoons cold water

- For the filling:
  - 2 cups cream cheese, softened
  - 3/4 cup granulated sugar
  - 2 large eggs
  - 1 teaspoon vanilla extract
  - 1/2 cup sour cream

- For the topping (optional):
  - Fresh berries
  - Whipped cream

Directions:

1. Preheat your oven to 350°F (175°C). Grease a 9-inch springform pan and set aside.

2. **For the crust:** In a food processor, combine einkorn flour, 1/4 cup sugar, and salt. Pulse to mix. Add chilled butter and pulse until the mixture resembles coarse crumbs. Gradually add cold water, 1 tablespoon at a time, pulsing until the dough starts to come together.

3. Press the dough into the bottom of the prepared springform pan, forming an even layer. Bake for 10 minutes, then remove from the oven and let cool.

4. **For the filling:** In a large bowl, beat the cream cheese and 3/4 cup sugar until smooth. Add eggs, one at a time, beating well after each addition. Mix in vanilla extract and sour cream until just combined.

5. Pour the filling over the cooled crust, smoothing the top with a spatula.

6. Bake for 45 minutes, or until the center is almost set but still slightly jiggly. Turn off the oven, open the oven door slightly, and let the cheesecake cool in the oven for 1 hour.

7. Remove from the oven and chill in the refrigerator for at least 4 hours, or overnight.

8. **For serving:** Release the cheesecake from the springform pan. Top with fresh berries and whipped cream if desired before serving.

Nutritional value per serving: Calories: 450, Carbs: 40g, Fiber: 1g, Sugars: 28g, Protein: 7g, Saturated fat: 18g, Unsaturated fat: 5g

Difficulty rating: Medium

Tips for ingredient variations:

- For a gluten-free version, substitute einkorn flour with your favorite gluten-free flour blend.

- Add 1 tablespoon of lemon zest to the filling for a citrusy twist.

- Replace fresh berries with a homemade einkorn flour crust for an added layer of flavor and texture.

48. Einkorn Peanut Butter Cookies

Number of servings: 24 cookies

Preparation time: 15 minutes

Cooking time: 10 minutes

Ingredients:

- 1 cup fresh-milled einkorn flour
- 1/2 teaspoon baking soda
- 1/4 teaspoon salt
- 1/2 cup unsalted butter, softened
- 3/4 cup creamy peanut butter
- 1/2 cup granulated sugar
- 1/2 cup packed brown sugar
- 1 large egg
- 1 teaspoon vanilla extract

Directions:

1. Preheat your oven to 375°F (190°C) and line two baking sheets with parchment paper.

2. In a small bowl, whisk together the fresh-milled einkorn flour, baking soda, and salt. Set aside.

3. In a large mixing bowl, beat together the softened butter, peanut butter, granulated sugar, and brown sugar until creamy and well combined.

4. Beat in the egg and vanilla extract until smooth.

5. Gradually add the dry ingredients to the wet ingredients, mixing until just combined.

6. Scoop tablespoon-sized balls of dough onto the prepared baking sheets, spacing them about 2 inches apart.

7. Bake in the preheated oven for 10 minutes, or until the edges are lightly golden and the centers appear set.

8. Allow the cookies to cool on the baking sheets for 5 minutes before transferring them to a wire rack to cool completely.

Nutritional value per serving: (per cookie)

- Calories: 140
- Carbs: 15g
- Fiber: 1g
- Sugars: 10g
- Protein: 3g
- Saturated fat: 3g
- Unsaturated fat: 2g

Difficulty rating: Easy

Tips for ingredient variations:

- For a crunchy texture, use crunchy peanut butter instead of creamy.

- Add 1/2 cup of chocolate chips or chopped nuts (such as peanuts or walnuts) to the dough for added flavor and texture.

- For a lower sugar option, reduce the granulated sugar to 1/4 cup and use a sugar substitute suitable for baking that measures like sugar.

49. Einkorn Cinnamon Coffee Cake

Number of servings: 12

Preparation time: 25 minutes

Cooking time: 45 minutes

Ingredients:

- For the cake:
  - 2 cups fresh-milled einkorn flour
  - 1 teaspoon baking powder
  - 1/2 teaspoon baking soda
  - 1/4 teaspoon salt
  - 1 tablespoon ground cinnamon
  - 1/2 cup unsalted butter, softened
  - 1 cup granulated sugar
  - 2 large eggs
  - 1 teaspoon vanilla extract
  - 1 cup sour cream
- For the topping:
  - 1/2 cup brown sugar, packed
  - 1 tablespoon ground cinnamon
  - 1/4 cup fresh-milled einkorn flour
  - 3 tablespoons unsalted butter, cold and cubed

Directions:

1. Preheat the oven to 350°F (175°C). Grease and flour a 9x13 inch baking pan.

2. In a medium bowl, whisk together 2 cups of einkorn flour, baking powder, baking soda, salt, and 1 tablespoon of cinnamon.

3. In a large bowl, cream together 1/2 cup of butter and granulated sugar until light and fluffy. Beat in the eggs, one at a time, then stir in the vanilla extract. Gradually add the flour mixture to the creamed mixture, alternating with sour cream, beginning and ending with the flour mixture. Mix until just combined.

4. Pour the batter into the prepared baking pan, spreading evenly.

5. To make the topping, in a small bowl, combine brown sugar, 1 tablespoon of cinnamon, and 1/4 cup of einkorn flour. Cut in 3 tablespoons of cold butter until the mixture resembles coarse crumbs. Sprinkle evenly over the batter in the pan.

6. Bake for 45 minutes, or until a toothpick inserted into the center comes out clean.

7. Allow to cool slightly before serving.

Nutritional value per serving: Calories: 320, Carbs: 45g, Fiber: 2g, Sugars: 28g, Protein: 4g, Saturated fat: 10g, Unsaturated fat: 3g

Difficulty rating: Medium

Tips for ingredient variations:

- For a dairy-free version, substitute the sour cream with a dairy-free yogurt and use a plant-based butter.

- Add 1/2 cup of chopped nuts (such as walnuts or pecans) to the topping for added texture.

- For an extra layer of flavor, mix 1/2 cup of raisins or finely chopped apples into the cake batter.

50. Einkorn Berry Tart

Number of servings: 8

Preparation time: 45 minutes

Cooking time: 25 minutes

Ingredients:

- For the crust:
  - 1 1/2 cups fresh-milled einkorn flour
  - 1/4 cup granulated sugar
  - 1/2 cup unsalted butter, chilled and cubed
  - 1/4 teaspoon salt
  - 2-3 tablespoons ice water
- For the filling:
  - 4 cups mixed fresh berries (such as strawberries, blueberries, raspberries, and blackberries)
  - 1/2 cup granulated sugar
  - 2 tablespoons fresh-milled einkorn flour
  - 1 tablespoon lemon juice
  - Zest of 1 lemon
- For the topping:
  - 1/2 cup fresh-milled einkorn flour
  - 1/4 cup granulated sugar
  - 1/4 cup unsalted butter, softened
  - 1/4 teaspoon ground cinnamon

Directions:

1. Preheat the oven to 375°F (190°C). Grease a 9-inch tart pan with a removable bottom.

2. For the crust, in a large bowl, combine einkorn flour, sugar, and salt. Add cubed butter and use a pastry blender or your fingers to mix until the mixture resembles coarse crumbs. Sprinkle ice water over the mixture, 1 tablespoon at a time, mixing until the dough just comes together. Press the dough into the prepared tart pan, evenly covering the bottom and sides. Chill in the refrigerator for 15 minutes.

3. Prick the crust all over with a fork, then bake for 15 minutes or until lightly golden. Remove from the oven and let cool slightly.

4. For the filling, in a large bowl, toss together the mixed berries, sugar, einkorn flour, lemon juice, and lemon zest. Spread the filling evenly over the pre-baked crust.

5. For the topping, in a small bowl, mix together einkorn flour, sugar, softened butter, and cinnamon until crumbly. Sprinkle this mixture over the berry filling.

6. Bake for 25 minutes, or until the topping is golden and the filling is bubbly. Let cool before removing from the tart pan.

Nutritional value per serving: Calories: 350, Carbs: 50g, Fiber: 4g, Sugars: 30g, Protein: 4g, Saturated fat: 10g, Unsaturated fat: 3g

Difficulty rating: Medium

Tips for ingredient variations:

- For a gluten-free version, substitute fresh-milled einkorn flour with a gluten-free all-purpose flour blend in equal amounts.

- Add a touch of nutmeg or allspice to the topping mixture for a spiced flavor.

- Substitute half of the granulated sugar in the filling with honey or maple syrup for a natural sweetness.

- For a dairy-free version, use plant-based butter in both the crust and topping.

51. Einkorn Chocolate Mousse

Number of servings: 4

Preparation time: 15 minutes

Cooking time: 0 minutes (Requires at least 2 hours of refrigeration)

Ingredients:

- 1/2 cup fresh-milled einkorn flour
- 2 tablespoons unsweetened cocoa powder
- 1/4 cup boiling water
- 1 teaspoon pure vanilla extract
- 1/4 cup honey
- 1 cup heavy cream, chilled
- A pinch of salt
- Dark chocolate shavings for garnish

Directions:

1. In a small bowl, whisk together the einkorn flour and unsweetened cocoa powder.

2. Gradually add the boiling water to the flour and cocoa mixture, whisking continuously until smooth.

3. Stir in the vanilla extract and honey until well combined. Allow the mixture to cool to room temperature.

4. In a separate bowl, beat the heavy cream with a pinch of salt until stiff peaks form.

5. Gently fold the cooled einkorn mixture into the whipped cream until no streaks remain, being careful not to deflate the cream.

6. Spoon the mousse into serving dishes and refrigerate for at least 2 hours, or until set.

7. Before serving, garnish with dark chocolate shavings.

Nutritional value per serving: Calories: 320, Carbs: 24g, Fiber: 2g, Sugars: 18g, Protein: 3g, Saturated fat: 18g, Unsaturated fat: 5g

Difficulty rating: Easy

Tips for ingredient variations:

- For a vegan version, substitute the heavy cream with chilled coconut cream and the honey with maple syrup.

- Add a tablespoon of espresso or strong coffee to the einkorn and cocoa mixture for a mocha flavor.

- For an extra rich mousse, fold in 1/4 cup of melted dark chocolate into the einkorn mixture before combining with the whipped cream.

52. Einkorn Pumpkin Pie

Number of servings: 8

Preparation time: 30 minutes

Cooking time: 55 minutes

Ingredients:

- For the crust:
  - 1 1/2 cups fresh-milled einkorn flour
  - 1/2 teaspoon salt
  - 1/2 cup unsalted butter, chilled and cubed
  - 4-5 tablespoons ice water
- For the filling:
  - 1 3/4 cups pumpkin puree
  - 3/4 cup granulated sugar
  - 1/2 teaspoon salt
  - 2 teaspoons ground cinnamon
  - 1 teaspoon ground ginger
  - 1/4 teaspoon ground cloves
  - 2 large eggs
  - 1 cup evaporated milk

Directions:

1. Start with the crust by combining the einkorn flour and salt in a large bowl. Add the chilled butter and use a pastry cutter or your fingers to mix until the mixture resembles coarse crumbs.

2. Gradually add ice water, one tablespoon at a time, mixing until the dough just begins to come together. Form the dough into a disk, wrap in plastic, and refrigerate for at least 1 hour.

3. Preheat the oven to 425°F (220°C). On a floured surface, roll out the dough into a 12-inch circle. Transfer to a 9-inch pie dish, trim any excess dough, and crimp the edges.

4. For the filling, mix the pumpkin puree, granulated sugar, salt, cinnamon, ginger, and cloves in a large bowl. Beat in the eggs, then gradually stir in the evaporated milk until well combined.

5. Pour the filling into the prepared crust and smooth the top with a spatula.

6. Bake in the preheated oven for 15 minutes. Reduce the oven temperature to 350°F (175°C) and continue baking for 40 minutes, or until a knife inserted near the center comes out clean.

7. Let the pie cool on a wire rack for 2 hours. Serve immediately or refrigerate.

Nutritional value per serving: Calories: 330, Carbs: 45g, Fiber: 2g, Sugars: 25g, Protein: 6g, Saturated fat: 10g, Unsaturated fat: 3g

Difficulty rating: Medium

Tips for ingredient variations:

- For a dairy-free version, substitute the butter in the crust with a plant-based alternative and use coconut milk instead of evaporated milk in the filling.

- Add a tablespoon of bourbon or dark rum to the filling for a deeper flavor.

- For a gluten-free crust, substitute einkorn flour with a gluten-free flour blend designed for pie crusts. Adjust the water as needed to achieve the right dough consistency.

53. Einkorn Lemon Pound Cake

Number of servings: 8 slices

Preparation time: 20 minutes

Cooking time: 50 minutes

Ingredients:

- 2 cups fresh-milled einkorn flour
- 1 teaspoon baking powder
- 1/2 teaspoon salt
- 1 cup unsalted butter, softened
- 1 cup granulated sugar
- 4 large eggs
- 1/4 cup lemon juice
- Zest of 2 lemons
- 1 teaspoon vanilla extract
- 1/2 cup buttermilk

For the Glaze:

- 1 cup powdered sugar
- 2 tablespoons lemon juice
- Zest of 1 lemon

Directions:

1. Preheat your oven to 350°F (175°C). Grease and flour a 9x5 inch loaf pan.

2. In a medium bowl, whisk together the fresh-milled einkorn flour, baking powder, and salt. Set aside.

3. In a large bowl, cream together the butter and granulated sugar until light and fluffy.

4. Beat in the eggs, one at a time, then stir in the lemon juice, lemon zest, and vanilla extract.

5. Gradually add the flour mixture to the wet ingredients, alternating with the buttermilk, beginning and ending with the flour mixture. Mix until just combined.

6. Pour the batter into the prepared loaf pan and smooth the top with a spatula.

7. Bake for 50 minutes, or until a toothpick inserted into the center comes out clean.

8. Allow the cake to cool in the pan for 10 minutes, then transfer to a wire rack to cool completely.

9. For the glaze, whisk together the powdered sugar, lemon juice, and lemon zest until smooth. Drizzle over the cooled cake.

Nutritional value per serving: Calories: 450, Carbs: 58g, Fiber: 1g, Sugars: 38g, Protein: 6g, Saturated fat: 15g, Unsaturated fat: 3g

Difficulty rating: Medium

Tips for ingredient variations:

- For a dairy-free version, substitute the buttermilk with almond milk mixed with 1 teaspoon of vinegar and use a plant-based butter.

- Add 1/2 cup of poppy seeds to the batter for a lemon poppy seed variation.

- For a less sweet cake, reduce the granulated sugar to 3/4 cup and omit the glaze.

54. Einkorn Linzer Cookies

Number of servings: 24 cookies

Preparation time: 45 minutes

Cooking time: 12 minutes per batch

Ingredients:

- 2 cups fresh-milled einkorn flour
- 1/2 teaspoon baking powder
- 1/4 teaspoon salt
- 1 cup unsalted butter, softened
- 2/3 cup granulated sugar
- 1 large egg
- 1 teaspoon vanilla extract
- 1/2 cup raspberry jam (for filling)
- Powdered sugar (for dusting)

Directions:

1. In a medium bowl, whisk together the fresh-milled einkorn flour, baking powder, and salt. Set aside.

2. In a large mixing bowl, cream together the softened butter and granulated sugar until light and fluffy. Beat in the egg and vanilla extract until well combined.

3. Gradually add the dry ingredients to the wet ingredients, mixing until a cohesive dough forms. Divide the dough in half, flatten into disks, wrap in plastic wrap, and chill in the refrigerator for at least 30 minutes.

4. Preheat your oven to 350°F (175°C). Line two baking sheets with parchment paper.

5. On a lightly floured surface, roll out one disk of dough to about 1/8-inch thickness. Use a 2-inch round cookie cutter to cut out cookies. Place half of the cookies on the prepared baking sheets.

6. Roll out the second disk of dough and cut out an equal number of cookies. Use a smaller cookie cutter or the end of a piping tip to cut a hole in the center of each cookie. These will serve as the top halves of your Linzer cookies.

7. Bake in the preheated oven for 10-12 minutes, or until the edges are lightly golden. Allow the cookies to cool on the baking sheets for 5 minutes before transferring them to a wire rack to cool completely.

8. Once cooled, spread a thin layer of raspberry jam on the whole cookies (without the hole). Dust the top halves (with the hole) lightly with powdered sugar, then place them on top of the jam-covered cookies to form sandwiches.

Nutritional value per serving: (per cookie)

- Calories: 150
- Carbs: 18g
- Fiber: 0.5g
- Sugars: 10g
- Protein: 2g
- Saturated fat: 5g
- Unsaturated fat: 2g

Difficulty rating: Medium

Tips for ingredient variations:

- Substitute raspberry jam with apricot, strawberry, or your favorite fruit jam.

- Add 1/2 teaspoon of almond extract to the dough for a nutty flavor.

- Mix in 1 teaspoon of lemon zest or orange zest to the dough for a citrusy twist.

- For a festive twist, mix in 1/4 teaspoon of ground cinnamon or nutmeg into the flour mixture.

55. Einkorn Coconut Macaroons

Nutritional value per serving: Calories: 120, Carbs: 15g, Fiber: 2g, Sugars: 10g, Protein: 2g, Saturated fat: 5g, Unsaturated fat: 0g

Difficulty rating: Easy

Tips for ingredient variations:

- For chocolate-dipped macaroons, melt 1/2 cup of dark chocolate chips in a microwave-safe bowl and dip the cooled macaroons halfway into the chocolate. Place them back on the parchment paper until the chocolate sets.

- Add 1/2 teaspoon almond extract to the mixture for an almond-flavored variation.

- For a lower sugar option, substitute granulated sugar with coconut sugar or a sugar alternative suitable for baking, adjusting the quantity to taste.

Number of servings: 24 macaroons

Preparation time: 15 minutes

Cooking time: 20 minutes

Ingredients:

- 3 cups shredded unsweetened coconut
- 1 cup fresh-milled einkorn flour
- 3/4 cup granulated sugar
- 1/4 teaspoon salt
- 4 large egg whites
- 1 teaspoon vanilla extract

Directions:

1. Preheat your oven to 325°F (163°C). Line two baking sheets with parchment paper.

2. In a large bowl, combine the shredded coconut, fresh-milled einkorn flour, granulated sugar, and salt.

3. Stir in the egg whites and vanilla extract until well mixed. The mixture should hold together when squeezed.

4. Using a tablespoon or a small ice cream scoop, form the mixture into small mounds and place them on the prepared baking sheets, spacing them about 1 inch apart.

5. Bake in the preheated oven for 20 minutes, or until the macaroons are golden around the edges.

6. Let the macaroons cool on the baking sheets for 5 minutes, then transfer them to a wire rack to cool completely.

56. Einkorn Shortbread Cookies

Number of servings: 24 cookies

Preparation time: 15 minutes

Cooking time: 12-15 minutes

Ingredients:

- 2 cups fresh-milled einkorn flour
- 1 cup unsalted butter, room temperature
- 1/2 cup powdered sugar, plus extra for dusting
- 1 teaspoon vanilla extract
- 1/4 teaspoon salt

Directions:

1. Preheat your oven to 350°F (175°C) and line two baking sheets with parchment paper.

2. In a large mixing bowl, cream together the butter and powdered sugar until light and fluffy.

3. Mix in the vanilla extract and salt.

4. Gradually add the fresh-milled einkorn flour to the butter mixture, stirring until well combined and a soft dough forms.

5. Roll the dough into 1-inch balls and place them on the prepared baking sheets, leaving about 2 inches between each cookie.

6. Gently flatten each ball with the bottom of a glass or your hand.

7. Bake in the preheated oven for 12-15 minutes, or until the edges are lightly golden.

8. Let the cookies cool on the baking sheets for 5 minutes, then transfer to a wire rack to cool completely.

9. Once cooled, dust the cookies with additional powdered sugar.

Nutritional value per serving: (per cookie)

- Calories: 110
- Carbs: 9g
- Fiber: 0.5g
- Sugars: 3g
- Protein: 1g
- Saturated fat: 5g
- Unsaturated fat: 2g

Difficulty rating: Easy

Tips for ingredient variations:

- For lemon-flavored cookies, add 1 tablespoon of lemon zest to the dough.

- Mix in 1/2 cup of finely chopped nuts such as pecans or walnuts for a crunchy texture.

- For a chocolate version, dip half of each cooled cookie into melted dark chocolate and place on parchment paper until set.

57. Einkorn Pecan Pie

Number of servings: 8

Preparation time: 30 minutes

Cooking time: 50 minutes

Ingredients:

- For the crust:
  - 1 1/2 cups fresh-milled einkorn flour
  - 1/2 teaspoon salt
  - 1/2 cup unsalted butter, chilled and diced
  - 4-5 tablespoons ice water
- For the filling:
  - 3 large eggs
  - 1 cup light corn syrup
  - 1/2 cup granulated sugar
  - 2 tablespoons unsalted butter, melted
  - 1 teaspoon vanilla extract
  - 1 1/2 cups pecan halves

Directions:

1. Start by making the crust. In a large bowl, combine the einkorn flour and salt. Cut in the chilled butter until the mixture resembles coarse crumbs. Gradually add ice water, stirring until the mixture forms a ball. Wrap in plastic and refrigerate for at least 30 minutes.

2. Preheat your oven to 350°F (175°C). On a floured surface, roll out the dough to fit a 9-inch pie plate. Transfer the crust to the pie plate and trim the edges.

3. For the filling, in a large bowl, beat the eggs lightly. Stir in the corn syrup, granulated sugar, melted butter, and vanilla extract until well blended. Mix in the pecan halves.

4. Pour the filling into the prepared crust. Bake in the preheated oven for 50 minutes, or until the filling is set and the crust is golden brown.

5. Let the pie cool on a wire rack before serving.

Nutritional value per serving: Calories: 520, Carbs: 68g, Fiber: 3g, Sugars: 48g, Protein: 6g, Saturated fat: 12g, Unsaturated fat: 9g

Difficulty rating: Medium

Tips for ingredient variations:

- For a healthier version, substitute the light corn syrup with maple syrup or honey. Adjust the sweetness according to taste.

- Add chocolate chips or chopped dark chocolate to the filling for a chocolate pecan pie variation.

- For a spicier pie, add 1/2 teaspoon of cinnamon or nutmeg to the filling mixture.

58. Einkorn Strawberry Shortcake

Number of servings: 8

Preparation time: 30 minutes

Cooking time: 15 minutes

Ingredients:
- For the shortcakes:
  - 2 cups fresh-milled einkorn flour
  - 1/4 cup granulated sugar
  - 1 tablespoon baking powder
  - 1/2 teaspoon salt
  - 1/2 cup cold unsalted butter, cubed
  - 3/4 cup whole milk
- For the filling:
  - 2 cups fresh strawberries, sliced
  - 2 tablespoons granulated sugar
- For the whipped cream:
  - 1 cup heavy cream
  - 1 tablespoon powdered sugar
  - 1 teaspoon vanilla extract

Directions:

1. Preheat the oven to 425°F (220°C). Line a baking sheet with parchment paper.

2. In a large bowl, whisk together einkorn flour, 1/4 cup granulated sugar, baking powder, and salt.

3. Add the cold butter to the flour mixture. Use a pastry blender or your fingers to cut the butter into the flour until the mixture resembles coarse crumbs.

4. Gradually pour in the milk, stirring just until the dough comes together.

5. Turn the dough out onto a floured surface and gently knead it a few times. Pat the dough into a 1-inch thick rectangle. Use a biscuit cutter to cut out 8 rounds. Place the rounds on the prepared baking sheet.

6. Bake for 15 minutes, or until the shortcakes are golden brown. Remove from the oven and let cool on a wire rack.

7. While the shortcakes are baking, prepare the filling by tossing the sliced strawberries with 2 tablespoons of granulated sugar. Set aside to macerate.

8. For the whipped cream, beat the heavy cream, powdered sugar, and vanilla extract in a bowl until stiff peaks form.

9. To assemble, split each shortcake in half horizontally. Spoon some of the macerated strawberries onto the bottom half of each shortcake. Add a dollop of whipped cream and then top with the other half of the shortcake. Serve immediately.

Nutritional value per serving: Calories: 420, Carbs: 45g, Fiber: 2g, Sugars: 18g, Protein: 5g, Saturated fat: 18g, Unsaturated fat: 5g

Difficulty rating: Medium

Tips for ingredient variations:

- Substitute strawberries with other fresh berries like blueberries or raspberries for a different flavor.

- Add a pinch of cinnamon or lemon zest to the shortcake dough for an extra layer of flavor.

- For a dairy-free version, use cold coconut oil instead of butter, almond milk instead of whole milk, and coconut cream for the whipped cream.

59. Einkorn Chocolate Eclairs

Number of servings: 12 eclairs

Preparation time: 1 hour 30 minutes

Cooking time: 30 minutes

Ingredients:

- For the choux pastry:
  - 1 cup water
  - 1/2 cup unsalted butter
  - 1 tablespoon sugar
  - 1/4 teaspoon salt
  - 1 cup fresh-milled einkorn flour
  - 4 large eggs
- For the filling:
  - 2 cups heavy cream
  - 1/4 cup powdered sugar
  - 1 teaspoon vanilla extract
- For the chocolate glaze:
  - 1/2 cup heavy cream
  - 4 ounces semi-sweet chocolate, chopped
  - 2 tablespoons unsalted butter
  - 1 tablespoon light corn syrup

Directions:

1. Preheat the oven to 425°F (220°C). Line a baking sheet with parchment paper.

2. In a medium saucepan, combine water, butter, sugar, and salt. Bring to a boil over medium heat.

3. Reduce heat to low and add the einkorn flour all at once, stirring vigorously until the mixture forms a ball and pulls away from the sides of the pan.

4. Transfer the dough to a mixing bowl and let cool for 5 minutes. Beat in the eggs, one at a time, until the mixture is smooth and glossy.

5. Spoon the dough into a piping bag fitted with a large round tip. Pipe 12 elongated shapes, about 4 inches long, onto the prepared baking sheet.

6. Bake for 15 minutes, then reduce the oven temperature to 375°F (190°C) and bake for an additional 15 minutes, or until the eclairs are golden brown. Remove from the oven and let cool on a wire rack.

7. For the filling, whip the heavy cream, powdered sugar, and vanilla extract in a bowl until stiff peaks form. Once the eclairs are cool, cut them in half horizontally and pipe or spoon the whipped cream into the bottoms of the eclairs.

8. For the chocolate glaze, heat the heavy cream in a small saucepan over medium heat until it begins to simmer. Remove from heat and add the chopped chocolate, butter, and corn syrup, stirring until smooth and glossy.

9. Dip the top halves of the eclairs into the chocolate glaze, then place them on top of the filled bottoms. Allow the glaze to set before serving.

Nutritional value per serving: Calories: 350, Carbs: 25g, Fiber: 1g, Sugars: 15g, Protein: 5g, Saturated fat: 20g, Unsaturated fat: 5g

Difficulty rating: Medium

Tips for ingredient variations:

- For a coffee-flavored filling, dissolve 1 tablespoon of instant coffee in the heavy cream before whipping.

- Add a pinch of cinnamon or nutmeg to the choux pastry dough for a spiced variation.

- Substitute dark chocolate for the semi-sweet chocolate in the glaze for a richer flavor.

60. Einkorn Banana Cream Pie

Number of servings: 8

Preparation time: 45 minutes

Cooking time: 30 minutes

Ingredients:

- **For the crust:**
  - 1 1/2 cups fresh-milled einkorn flour
  - 1/4 teaspoon salt
  - 1/2 cup unsalted butter, chilled and cubed
  - 4-5 tablespoons ice water

- **For the filling:**
  - 3 large bananas, sliced
  - 1/3 cup granulated sugar
  - 2 tablespoons fresh-milled einkorn flour
  - 1/4 teaspoon salt
  - 1 1/2 cups whole milk
  - 3 large egg yolks, lightly beaten
  - 2 tablespoons unsalted butter
  - 1 teaspoon vanilla extract

- **For the topping:**
  - 1 cup heavy cream
  - 2 tablespoons confectioners' sugar
  - 1/2 teaspoon vanilla extract
  - Additional banana slices for garnish

Directions:

1. **For the crust:** In a mixing bowl, combine einkorn flour and salt. Cut in the butter until the mixture resembles coarse crumbs. Gradually add ice water, stirring until the mixture forms a ball. Wrap in plastic and refrigerate for at least 30 minutes.

2. Preheat oven to 375°F (190°C). Roll out the dough on a floured surface to fit a 9-inch pie plate. Transfer crust to pie plate. Prick the bottom with a fork. Bake for 25-30 minutes or until golden. Cool completely.

3. **For the filling:** Arrange banana slices in the cooled crust. In a saucepan, mix sugar, einkorn flour, and salt. Gradually stir in milk. Cook over medium heat, stirring constantly, until thickened and bubbly. Reduce heat; cook and stir 2 minutes more.

4. Remove from heat. Gradually stir 1 cup of the hot filling into egg yolks, then return all to the saucepan. Bring to a gentle boil; cook and stir for 2 more minutes. Remove from heat; stir in butter and vanilla. Cool to room temperature without stirring.

5. Pour filling over banana slices in crust. Cover and chill for at least 2 hours until set.

6. **For the topping:** In a mixing bowl, beat heavy cream, confectioners' sugar, and vanilla extract until stiff peaks form. Spread over pie. Garnish with additional banana slices.

Nutritional value per serving: Calories: 450, Carbs: 40g, Fiber: 2g, Sugars: 20g, Protein: 5g, Saturated fat: 18g, Unsaturated fat: 5g

Difficulty rating: Medium

Tips for ingredient variations:

- For a gluten-free version, substitute einkorn flour with your favorite gluten-free flour blend in both crust and filling. Adjust the amount of water as needed for the crust.

- Add a layer of chocolate ganache under the banana layer for a decadent twist. Melt 1/2 cup of chocolate chips with 1/4 cup of heavy cream and spread over the cooled crust before adding bananas.

- For a dairy-free version, use coconut oil instead of butter in the crust, full-fat coconut milk in the filling, and coconut cream for the topping.

Chapter 5: 20 Savory Snacks

61. Einkorn Cheese Crackers

Number of servings: 24 crackers

Preparation time: 15 minutes

Cooking time: 12-15 minutes

Ingredients:

- 1 cup fresh-milled einkorn flour
- 1/2 teaspoon salt
- 1/2 teaspoon baking powder
- 4 tablespoons unsalted butter, cold and cubed
- 1 cup sharp cheddar cheese, grated
- 2-4 tablespoons ice water
- 1/2 teaspoon paprika (optional for added flavor)
- Coarse sea salt for topping

Directions:

1. Preheat your oven to 350°F (175°C) and line a baking sheet with parchment paper.

2. In a large bowl, whisk together the einkorn flour, salt, and baking powder.

3. Add the cold, cubed butter to the flour mixture. Use a pastry blender or your fingers to cut the butter into the flour until the mixture resembles coarse crumbs.

4. Stir in the grated cheddar cheese and paprika (if using) until evenly distributed.

5. Gradually add ice water, one tablespoon at a time, mixing until the dough comes together in a ball. You may not need all the water, so add it slowly until the dough is the right consistency.

6. On a lightly floured surface, roll out the dough to about 1/8 inch thickness. Use a cookie cutter or knife to cut the dough into desired shapes.

7. Place the cutouts on the prepared baking sheet and sprinkle with coarse sea salt.

8. Bake in the preheated oven for 12-15 minutes, or until the crackers are lightly golden and crispy.

9. Remove from the oven and let cool on the baking sheet for 5 minutes before transferring to a wire rack to cool completely.

Nutritional value per serving:

- Calories: 70
- Carbs: 4g
- Fiber: 0.5g
- Sugars: 0g
- Protein: 2g
- Saturated fat: 2g
- Unsaturated fat: 1g

Difficulty rating: Easy

Tips for ingredient variations:

- For a spicier cracker, add 1/4 teaspoon of cayenne pepper to the dough.

- Substitute sharp cheddar cheese with Parmesan or Gouda for a different flavor profile.

- Add 1 tablespoon of fresh herbs, such as rosemary or thyme, finely chopped, to the dough for an aromatic twist.

62. Einkorn Herb Crackers

Number of servings: 24 crackers

Preparation time: 20 minutes

Cooking time: 12 minutes

Ingredients:

- 1 1/2 cups fresh-milled einkorn flour
- 1 teaspoon sugar
- 1/2 teaspoon salt
- 2 tablespoons olive oil
- 1/2 cup water
- 1 tablespoon fresh rosemary, finely chopped
- 1 tablespoon fresh thyme, finely chopped
- Coarse sea salt for sprinkling

Directions:

1. Preheat your oven to 450°F (232°C) and line a baking sheet with parchment paper.
2. In a large mixing bowl, combine the einkorn flour, sugar, and 1/2 teaspoon salt.
3. Add the olive oil and water to the flour mixture. Stir until a dough forms.
4. Mix in the chopped rosemary and thyme until evenly distributed throughout the dough.
5. Turn the dough out onto a floured surface and roll it out to about 1/8 inch thickness.
6. Cut the dough into rectangles or desired shapes using a knife or cookie cutter and place them on the prepared baking sheet.
7. Prick each cracker a few times with a fork to prevent puffing during baking.
8. Sprinkle the crackers with coarse sea salt.
9. Bake in the preheated oven for 10-12 minutes, or until the edges are lightly golden.
10. Remove from the oven and let the crackers cool on the baking sheet for 5 minutes before transferring them to a wire rack to cool completely.

Nutritional value per serving:

- Calories: 45
- Carbs: 6g
- Fiber: 1g
- Sugars: 0g
- Protein: 1g
- Saturated fat: 0g
- Unsaturated fat: 1g

Difficulty rating: Easy

Tips for ingredient variations:

- Substitute rosemary and thyme with any other herbs you prefer, such as oregano or basil, for a different flavor profile.

- Add 1/4 cup of grated Parmesan cheese to the dough for a cheesy twist.

- For a spicier cracker, mix in 1/2 teaspoon of red pepper flakes.

63. Einkorn Pretzel Bites

Number of servings: 24 bites

Preparation time: 1 hour 30 minutes

Cooking time: 15 minutes

Ingredients:

- 1 1/2 cups warm water (110°F)
- 1 tablespoon sugar
- 2 teaspoons active dry yeast
- 4 1/2 cups fresh-milled einkorn flour, plus more for dusting
- 2 teaspoons salt
- 4 tablespoons unsalted butter, melted
- 10 cups water for boiling
- 2/3 cup baking soda
- Coarse sea salt for topping

Directions:

1. Combine warm water, sugar, and yeast in a large bowl. Let sit for 5 minutes until the mixture becomes frothy.

2. Add 4 1/2 cups of fresh-milled einkorn flour, salt, and melted butter to the yeast mixture. Mix until a dough forms.

3. Knead the dough on a lightly floured surface for about 5 minutes until smooth and elastic. Place the dough in a greased bowl, cover with a cloth, and let rise in a warm place for 1 hour or until doubled in size.

4. Preheat the oven to 425°F (218°C). Line two baking sheets with parchment paper.

5. Bring 10 cups of water to a boil in a large pot. Gradually add baking soda.

6. Turn the risen dough out onto a lightly floured surface. Divide into 24 equal pieces. Roll each piece into a ball, then into a rope about 1/2 inch thick and 6 inches long. Twist each rope into a pretzel shape.

7. Boil the pretzels in the baking soda water for 30 seconds each, then place on the prepared baking sheets.

8. Sprinkle the boiled pretzels with coarse sea salt.

9. Bake for 12-15 minutes or until golden brown.

10. Let cool on a wire rack before serving.

Nutritional value per serving:

- Calories: 150
- Carbs: 27g
- Fiber: 1g
- Sugars: 1g
- Protein: 4g
- Saturated fat: 1g
- Unsaturated fat: 1g

Difficulty rating: Medium

Tips for ingredient variations:

- For a cheesy twist, sprinkle grated Parmesan or cheddar cheese over the pretzels before baking.

- Add dried herbs such as rosemary or thyme to the dough for an aromatic flavor.

- For a sweet version, omit the coarse salt topping and instead brush with melted butter and sprinkle with cinnamon sugar after baking.

64. Einkorn Parmesan Breadsticks

Number of servings: 24 breadsticks

Preparation time: 20 minutes

Cooking time: 15 minutes

Ingredients:

- 2 1/2 cups fresh-milled einkorn flour
- 1 tablespoon active dry yeast
- 1 teaspoon sugar
- 1 cup warm water (about 110°F)
- 2 tablespoons olive oil
- 2 garlic cloves, minced
- 1 teaspoon salt
- 1 tablespoon dried Italian herbs (such as a mix of oregano, basil, and thyme)
- 1/4 cup unsalted butter, melted
- Coarse sea salt for sprinkling
- 1/2 cup grated Parmesan cheese

Directions:

1. In a small bowl, dissolve the yeast and sugar in warm water. Let it sit for 5 minutes until frothy.
2. In a large mixing bowl, combine the fresh-milled einkorn flour, minced garlic, salt, and dried Italian herbs.
3. Add the yeast mixture and olive oil to the flour mixture. Stir until a dough forms.
4. Turn the dough out onto a floured surface and knead for about 5 minutes, until smooth and elastic. Add more flour if the dough is too sticky.
5. Place the dough in a greased bowl, cover with a clean cloth, and let it rise in a warm place for about 1 hour, or until doubled in size.
6. Preheat your oven to 425°F (220°C). Line a baking sheet with parchment paper.
7. Punch down the dough and turn it out onto a floured surface. Divide the dough into 24 equal pieces.
8. Roll each piece into a rope about 8 inches long. Place the ropes on the prepared baking sheet, leaving space between each.
9. Brush the tops of the breadsticks with melted butter and sprinkle with coarse sea salt and grated Parmesan cheese.
10. Bake in the preheated oven for 15 minutes, or until golden brown.
11. Remove from the oven and let cool slightly on a wire rack before serving.

Nutritional value per serving:

- Calories: 110
- Carbs: 15g
- Fiber: 1g
- Sugars: 0.5g
- Protein: 3g
- Saturated fat: 2g
- Unsaturated fat: 1g

Difficulty rating: Easy

Tips for ingredient variations:

- For a garlic butter version, mix additional minced garlic into the melted butter before brushing it on the breadsticks.
- Substitute the Italian herbs with rosemary or thyme for a different flavor profile.
- For a vegan option, use a plant-based butter substitute and omit the Parmesan cheese or use a vegan Parmesan alternative.

65. Einkorn Spinach and Feta Puffs

Number of servings: 12 puffs

Preparation time: 20 minutes

Cooking time: 25 minutes

Ingredients:

- 1 cup fresh-milled einkorn flour
- 1 cup water
- 1/2 cup unsalted butter
- 1/2 teaspoon salt
- 4 large eggs
- 1 cup spinach, finely chopped
- 1/2 cup feta cheese, crumbled
- 1 teaspoon garlic powder
- 1 tablespoon olive oil

Directions:

1. Preheat the oven to 425°F (220°C) and line a baking sheet with parchment paper.

2. In a medium saucepan, combine water, butter, and salt. Bring to a boil over medium heat.

3. Reduce the heat to low and add the fresh-milled einkorn flour, stirring vigorously until the mixture forms a ball and pulls away from the sides of the pan.

4. Transfer the dough to a mixing bowl and let it cool for a few minutes. Beat in the eggs, one at a time, ensuring each is fully incorporated before adding the next.

5. Stir in the spinach, feta cheese, and garlic powder until evenly distributed.

6. Using a tablespoon, drop spoonfuls of the dough onto the prepared baking sheet, spacing them about 2 inches apart.

7. Bake in the preheated oven for 20-25 minutes, or until the puffs are golden brown and puffed up.

8. Brush the warm puffs with olive oil before serving.

Nutritional value per serving:

- Calories: 150
- Carbs: 8g
- Fiber: 1g
- Sugars: 0g
- Protein: 4g
- Saturated fat: 5g
- Unsaturated fat: 2g

Difficulty rating: Medium

Tips for ingredient variations:

- Substitute spinach with kale or Swiss chard for a different green option.

- Add 1/4 cup of cooked, crumbled bacon or sausage for a meaty version.

- For a spicier puff, include 1/2 teaspoon of red pepper flakes in the dough.

66. Einkorn Garlic Knots

Number of servings: 24 knots

Preparation time: 2 hours (including dough rising time)

Cooking time: 15 minutes

Ingredients:

- 3 1/2 cups fresh-milled einkorn flour
- 1 tablespoon active dry yeast
- 1 teaspoon sugar
- 1 1/4 cups warm water (110°F)
- 2 tablespoons olive oil
- 2 teaspoons salt
- 3 cloves garlic, minced
- 1/4 cup unsalted butter, melted
- 2 tablespoons fresh parsley, chopped
- Coarse salt, for sprinkling

Directions:

1. In a small bowl, dissolve the yeast and sugar in warm water. Let it sit until frothy, about 5-10 minutes.

2. In a large mixing bowl, combine the fresh-milled einkorn flour and salt. Add the yeast mixture and olive oil. Mix until a soft dough forms.

3. Turn the dough out onto a floured surface and knead for about 10 minutes, until smooth and elastic.

4. Place the dough in a greased bowl, turning once to coat. Cover with a damp cloth and let rise in a warm place for about 1 hour, or until doubled in size.

5. Preheat your oven to 400°F (200°C). Line a baking sheet with parchment paper.

6. Punch down the dough and turn it out onto a floured surface. Divide the dough into 24 equal pieces.

7. Roll each piece into a 6-inch rope, then tie into a knot. Place the knots on the prepared baking sheet.

8. In a small saucepan, melt the butter over low heat. Add the minced garlic and cook for 1-2 minutes, until fragrant. Remove from heat and stir in the chopped parsley.

9. Brush the garlic butter mixture over the knots and sprinkle with coarse salt.

10. Bake for 15 minutes, or until golden brown.

11. Serve warm.

Nutritional value per serving:

- Calories: 120
- Carbs: 18g
- Fiber: 2g
- Sugars: 0.5g
- Protein: 3g
- Saturated fat: 2g
- Unsaturated fat: 1g

Difficulty rating: Medium

Tips for ingredient variations:

- For a dairy-free version, use olive oil instead of butter for the garlic topping.

- Add grated Parmesan cheese to the garlic butter mixture for a cheesy flavor.

- For an extra kick, include 1/2 teaspoon of red pepper flakes in the garlic butter mixture.

67. Einkorn Jalapeño Cornbread Muffins

Number of servings: 12 muffins

Preparation time: 20 minutes

Cooking time: 25 minutes

Ingredients:

- 1 1/2 cups fresh-milled einkorn flour
- 1/2 cup yellow cornmeal
- 1/4 cup granulated sugar
- 2 teaspoons baking powder
- 1/2 teaspoon salt
- 1 cup buttermilk
- 1/4 cup unsalted butter, melted
- 2 large eggs
- 2 jalapeños, seeded and finely chopped
- 1/2 cup shredded sharp cheddar cheese

Directions:

1. Preheat your oven to 375°F (190°C). Grease or line a 12-cup muffin tin with paper liners.

2. In a large bowl, whisk together the fresh-milled einkorn flour, cornmeal, sugar, baking powder, and salt.

3. In a separate bowl, whisk together the buttermilk, melted butter, and eggs until well combined.

4. Pour the wet ingredients into the dry ingredients and stir until just combined. Avoid overmixing.

5. Fold in the chopped jalapeños and shredded cheddar cheese until evenly distributed throughout the batter.

6. Divide the batter evenly among the prepared muffin cups, filling each about 3/4 full.

7. Bake in the preheated oven for 20-25 minutes, or until a toothpick inserted into the center of a muffin comes out clean.

8. Let the muffins cool in the pan for 5 minutes before transferring them to a wire rack to cool completely.

Nutritional value per serving:

- Calories: 180
- Carbs: 22g
- Fiber: 1g
- Sugars: 5g
- Protein: 5g
- Saturated fat: 3g
- Unsaturated fat: 1g

Difficulty rating: Easy

Tips for ingredient variations:

- For a spicier kick, leave some seeds in the jalapeños or add an extra jalapeño.

- Substitute buttermilk with 1 cup of milk mixed with 1 tablespoon of vinegar or lemon juice if buttermilk is not available.

- Add 1/2 cup of corn kernels to the batter for extra texture and sweetness.

- For a gluten-free version, substitute fresh-milled einkorn flour with your preferred gluten-free flour blend, adjusting the amount if necessary to achieve the right batter consistency.

68. Einkorn Onion Rings

Number of servings: 4

Preparation time: 20 minutes

Cooking time: 5 minutes

Ingredients:

- 1 large onion, sliced into 1/4-inch rings
- 1 cup fresh-milled einkorn flour
- 1 teaspoon baking powder
- 1/2 teaspoon salt
- 1 egg, beaten
- 1 cup milk
- Bread crumbs for coating
- Vegetable oil for frying

Directions:

1. Separate the onion slices into rings, and set aside.

2. In a mixing bowl, combine the fresh-milled einkorn flour, baking powder, and salt.

3. Stir in the beaten egg and milk into the flour mixture until a smooth batter is formed.

4. Place the bread crumbs in a shallow dish.

5. Heat the vegetable oil in a deep fryer or large saucepan to 375°F (190°C).

6. Dip each onion ring into the batter, then dredge in the bread crumbs, ensuring each ring is fully coated.

7. Carefully drop the coated onion rings into the hot oil and fry for 2-3 minutes or until golden brown.

8. Remove the onion rings with a slotted spoon and drain on paper towels to remove excess oil.

Nutritional value per serving:

- Calories: 280
- Carbs: 45g
- Fiber: 2g
- Sugars: 6g
- Protein: 8g
- Saturated fat: 2g
- Unsaturated fat: 5g

Difficulty rating: Easy

Tips for ingredient variations:

- For a gluten-free version, substitute the einkorn flour with a gluten-free flour blend.

- Add spices such as paprika, garlic powder, or cayenne pepper to the batter for extra flavor.

- For a dairy-free option, use almond milk or another plant-based milk in place of regular milk.

69. Einkorn Savory Hand Pies

Number of servings: 8

Preparation time: 45 minutes

Cooking time: 25 minutes

Ingredients:

- For the dough:
  - 2 cups fresh-milled einkorn flour
  - 1/4 teaspoon salt
  - 1/2 cup unsalted butter, chilled and cubed
  - 4-6 tablespoons ice water
- For the filling:
  - 1 tablespoon olive oil
  - 1 small onion, finely chopped
  - 1 garlic clove, minced
  - 1 cup spinach, chopped
  - 1/2 cup ricotta cheese
  - 1/4 cup feta cheese, crumbled
  - Salt and pepper to taste
  - 1 egg, beaten (for egg wash)

Directions:

1. In a large mixing bowl, combine the einkorn flour and salt. Add the cubed butter and use a pastry blender or two forks to cut the butter into the flour until the mixture resembles coarse crumbs.

2. Gradually add ice water, one tablespoon at a time, mixing with a fork until the dough comes together. Form into a disk, wrap in plastic wrap, and refrigerate for at least 30 minutes.

3. Preheat the oven to 375°F (190°C). Line a baking sheet with parchment paper.

4. Heat olive oil in a skillet over medium heat. Add onion and garlic, sautéing until softened, about 5 minutes. Add spinach and cook until wilted. Remove from heat and let cool.

5. In a bowl, mix the cooled spinach mixture with ricotta and feta cheese. Season with salt and pepper.

6. Roll out the chilled dough on a floured surface to about 1/8-inch thickness. Cut into 8 circles using a 4-inch cookie cutter or a cup.

7. Place a spoonful of the filling on one half of each circle. Fold the dough over the filling to create a half-moon shape. Press the edges to seal, then crimp with a fork.

8. Place the hand pies on the prepared baking sheet. Brush the tops with beaten egg.

9. Bake for 25 minutes, or until golden brown. Let cool slightly before serving.

Nutritional value per serving: Calories: 280, Carbs: 22g, Fiber: 2g, Sugars: 1g, Protein: 7g, Saturated fat: 10g, Unsaturated fat: 3g

Difficulty rating: Medium

Tips for ingredient variations:

- Substitute spinach with kale or Swiss chard for a different green.

- Add cooked, crumbled bacon or sausage to the filling for a meaty version.

- For a vegan hand pie, replace ricotta and feta with mashed tofu seasoned with nutritional yeast, and use a vegan egg wash substitute.

70. Einkorn Cheddar Scones

Number of servings: 8 scones

Preparation time: 20 minutes

Cooking time: 22 minutes

Ingredients:

- 2 cups fresh-milled einkorn flour
- 1 tablespoon baking powder
- 1/2 teaspoon salt
- 1/4 teaspoon black pepper
- 1/2 cup cold unsalted butter, cubed
- 3/4 cup shredded sharp cheddar cheese
- 1/4 cup finely chopped fresh chives
- 3/4 cup heavy cream, plus more for brushing

Directions:

1. Preheat the oven to 425°F (218°C). Line a baking sheet with parchment paper.

2. In a large bowl, whisk together the einkorn flour, baking powder, salt, and black pepper.

3. Add the cold butter to the flour mixture. Use a pastry blender or your fingers to cut the butter into the flour until the mixture resembles coarse crumbs.

4. Stir in the shredded cheddar cheese and chopped chives.

5. Gradually add the heavy cream, stirring until the dough begins to come together.

6. Turn the dough out onto a lightly floured surface and knead gently until it forms a cohesive mass. Do not over-knead.

7. Pat the dough into a circle about 1 inch thick. Use a sharp knife or dough cutter to cut the circle into 8 equal wedges.

8. Place the scones on the prepared baking sheet, leaving a few inches between each for expansion. Brush the tops of the scones with a little extra heavy cream.

9. Bake in the preheated oven for 20-22 minutes, or until the scones are golden brown and a toothpick inserted into the center comes out clean.

10. Remove from the oven and let cool on the baking sheet for 5 minutes before transferring to a wire rack to cool completely.

Nutritional value per serving: Calories: 350, Carbs: 28g, Fiber: 1g, Sugars: 1g, Protein: 7g, Saturated fat: 15g, Unsaturated fat: 5g

Difficulty rating: Easy

Tips for ingredient variations:

- Substitute the cheddar cheese with any other hard cheese of your preference for a different flavor profile.

- Add 1/2 cup of cooked and crumbled bacon or ham to the dough for a meaty version.

- For a spicier scone, include 1/4 teaspoon of cayenne pepper or 1/2 teaspoon of dried mustard in the dry ingredients.

71. Einkorn Savory Pinwheels

Number of servings: 12 pinwheels

Preparation time: 25 minutes

Cooking time: 20 minutes

Ingredients:

- 2 cups fresh-milled einkorn flour
- 1 tablespoon baking powder
- 1/2 teaspoon salt
- 1/2 cup cold unsalted butter, cubed
- 3/4 cup whole milk
- 1 cup grated sharp cheddar cheese
- 1/2 cup finely chopped cooked ham
- 1/4 cup finely chopped green onions
- 1 egg, beaten (for egg wash)

Directions:

1. Preheat your oven to 400°F (200°C) and line a baking sheet with parchment paper.

2. In a large mixing bowl, whisk together the einkorn flour, baking powder, and salt.

3. Cut in the cold butter using a pastry blender or two forks until the mixture resembles coarse crumbs.

4. Gradually add the milk, stirring until the dough comes together.

5. Turn the dough out onto a floured surface and knead gently until smooth, about 1-2 minutes.

6. Roll the dough into a 12x10 inch rectangle.

7. Sprinkle the grated cheese, ham, and green onions evenly over the dough.

8. Starting with the long side, roll the dough tightly into a log.

9. Cut the log into 12 equal slices and place them cut side down on the prepared baking sheet.

10. Brush the tops of the pinwheels with the beaten egg.

11. Bake for 20 minutes, or until golden brown.

12. Remove from the oven and let cool slightly on a wire rack before serving.

Nutritional value per serving:

- Calories: 220
- Carbs: 18g
- Fiber: 1g
- Sugars: 1g
- Protein: 7g
- Saturated fat: 5g
- Unsaturated fat: 2g

Difficulty rating: Medium

Tips for ingredient variations:

- Substitute the ham with cooked bacon or sausage for a different flavor.

- Add a teaspoon of dried herbs, such as thyme or rosemary, to the dough for an aromatic twist.

- For a vegetarian version, replace the ham with sautéed mushrooms or spinach.

72. Einkorn Tomato Basil Tartlets

Number of servings: 12 tartlets

Preparation time: 45 minutes

Cooking time: 25 minutes

Ingredients:

- For the crust:
  - 1 1/2 cups fresh-milled einkorn flour
  - 1/2 teaspoon salt
  - 1/2 cup unsalted butter, chilled and cubed
  - 3-4 tablespoons ice water
- For the filling:
  - 1 cup ricotta cheese
  - 1/4 cup grated Parmesan cheese
  - 1 egg
  - 1 tablespoon fresh basil, chopped
  - 1/2 teaspoon salt
  - 1/4 teaspoon black pepper
  - 2 tomatoes, thinly sliced
  - Additional basil leaves for garnish

Directions:

1. Preheat the oven to 375°F (190°C). In a mixing bowl, combine einkorn flour and salt. Add cubed butter and use a pastry blender or fingers to incorporate until the mixture resembles coarse crumbs. Gradually add ice water, stirring until the dough comes together.

2. Divide the dough into 12 equal portions. Press each portion into the bottom and up the sides of a muffin tin, forming a small tart shell. Prick the bottom of each shell with a fork. Bake for 10 minutes, then remove from oven and let cool slightly.

3. In a bowl, mix ricotta cheese, Parmesan cheese, egg, chopped basil, salt, and pepper until well combined.

4. Spoon the cheese mixture into each tart shell. Top with tomato slices.

5. Bake for an additional 15 minutes, or until the filling is set and the crust is golden brown.

6. Let tartlets cool for 5 minutes before removing from the tin. Garnish with additional basil leaves before serving.

Nutritional value per serving: Calories: 200, Carbs: 15g, Fiber: 1g, Sugars: 1g, Protein: 6g, Saturated fat: 5g, Unsaturated fat: 3g

Difficulty rating: Medium

Tips for ingredient variations:

- Swap ricotta cheese with goat cheese for a tangier flavor.

- Add sautéed spinach or mushrooms to the filling for extra vegetables.

- For a gluten-free crust, substitute einkorn flour with a gluten-free flour blend, adjusting the amount of water as needed to achieve the right dough consistency.

73. Einkorn Stuffed Breadsticks

Number of servings: 12 breadsticks

Preparation time: 20 minutes

Cooking time: 15 minutes

Ingredients:

- 2 cups fresh-milled einkorn flour
- 1 tablespoon active dry yeast
- 1 teaspoon sugar
- 1 teaspoon salt
- 3/4 cup warm water
- 2 tablespoons olive oil
- 1/2 cup grated Parmesan cheese
- 1/4 cup finely chopped fresh herbs (such as rosemary, thyme, and oregano)
- 1/2 cup mozzarella cheese, cut into 12 small cubes
- 1 egg, beaten (for egg wash)
- Coarse sea salt, for sprinkling

Directions:

1. In a large mixing bowl, combine the einkorn flour, active dry yeast, sugar, and salt.

2. Add the warm water and olive oil to the flour mixture. Mix until a soft dough forms.

3. Turn the dough out onto a floured surface and knead for about 5 minutes, until smooth.

4. Roll the dough into a 12x8 inch rectangle. Sprinkle the grated Parmesan and chopped herbs evenly over the dough.

5. Cut the dough into 12 strips, each 1 inch wide.

6. Place a cube of mozzarella cheese at the end of each strip. Roll the dough around the cheese, sealing the ends to enclose the cheese completely.

7. Place the stuffed breadsticks on a baking sheet lined with parchment paper. Cover and let rise in a warm place for 10 minutes.

8. Preheat the oven to 375°F (190°C).

9. Brush the breadsticks with the beaten egg and sprinkle with coarse sea salt.

10. Bake for 15 minutes, or until golden brown.

11. Remove from the oven and let cool slightly before serving.

Nutritional value per serving: Calories: 150, Carbs: 20g, Fiber: 2g, Sugars: 1g, Protein: 6g, Saturated fat: 2g, Unsaturated fat: 3g

Difficulty rating: Medium

Tips for ingredient variations:

- Substitute the mozzarella cheese with cheddar or pepper jack for a different flavor.

- Add minced garlic or garlic powder to the dough for a garlic twist.

- For a vegan version, use vegan cheese alternatives and brush the breadsticks with olive oil instead of an egg wash.

74. Einkorn Olive Tapenade Rolls

Number of servings: 12 rolls

Preparation time: 2 hours

Cooking time: 25 minutes

Ingredients:

- 1 1/2 cups warm water (110°F)

- 1 tablespoon sugar

- 2 teaspoons active dry yeast

- 3 1/2 cups fresh-milled einkorn flour, plus more for dusting

- 2 tablespoons olive oil, plus extra for greasing

- 1 teaspoon salt

- 1 cup olive tapenade

Directions:

1. In a small bowl, dissolve the sugar in warm water. Sprinkle the yeast over the top and let sit for 5 minutes, or until foamy.

2. In a large mixing bowl, combine the fresh-milled einkorn flour and salt. Make a well in the center and add the yeast mixture and olive oil.

3. Mix until a sticky dough forms. Turn out onto a floured surface and knead for about 10 minutes, until smooth and elastic. Add more flour as needed to prevent sticking.

4. Place the dough in a greased bowl, turning once to coat. Cover with a clean towel and let rise in a warm place for about 1 hour, or until doubled in size.

5. Punch down the dough and turn it out onto a floured surface. Divide into 12 equal pieces.

6. Roll each piece into a ball, then flatten into a disc. Spread about 1 tablespoon of olive tapenade over each disc, leaving a small border around the edge.

7. Roll up each disc tightly to enclose the tapenade. Place the rolls seam-side down on a greased baking sheet.

8. Cover and let rise for another 30 minutes, or until puffed up.

9. Preheat the oven to 375°F (190°C).

10. Bake the rolls for 25 minutes, or until golden brown on top.

11. Remove from the oven and let cool on a wire rack before serving.

Nutritional value per serving: Calories: 220, Carbs: 35g, Fiber: 4g, Sugars: 1g, Protein: 5g, Saturated fat: 0.5g, Unsaturated fat: 3g

Difficulty rating: Medium

Tips for ingredient variations:

- Substitute olive tapenade with sun-dried tomato pesto for a different flavor profile.

- Add grated Parmesan cheese or finely chopped fresh herbs (such as rosemary or thyme) into the dough for an extra layer of taste.

- For a spicier kick, mix a small amount of crushed red pepper flakes into the olive tapenade before spreading on the dough.

75. Einkorn Zucchini Fritters

Number of servings: 4

Preparation time: 20 minutes

Cooking time: 10 minutes

Ingredients:

- 1 cup fresh-milled einkorn flour
- 2 medium zucchinis, grated
- 1/4 cup grated Parmesan cheese
- 2 large eggs, beaten
- 1/2 teaspoon garlic powder
- Salt and pepper to taste
- 2 tablespoons olive oil for frying

Directions:

1. Place the grated zucchini in a colander, sprinkle with salt, and let it sit for 10 minutes to draw out moisture. Squeeze the excess water from the zucchini.

2. In a large bowl, combine the drained zucchini, fresh-milled einkorn flour, grated Parmesan cheese, beaten eggs, garlic powder, and season with salt and pepper. Stir until well mixed.

3. Heat olive oil in a large skillet over medium heat.

4. Scoop 1/4 cup of the zucchini mixture into the skillet, flattening with the back of the scoop to form a fritter. Cook for about 5 minutes on each side, or until golden brown and crispy.

5. Transfer the cooked fritters to a paper towel-lined plate to drain any excess oil.

6. Serve warm.

Nutritional value per serving:

- Calories: 220
- Carbs: 18g
- Fiber: 3g
- Sugars: 2g
- Protein: 9g
- Saturated fat: 3g
- Unsaturated fat: 4g

Difficulty rating: Easy

Tips for ingredient variations:

- For a gluten-free version, ensure your einkorn flour is certified gluten-free or substitute with another gluten-free flour of your choice.

- Add chopped fresh herbs such as parsley or dill to the mixture for added flavor.

- For a vegan version, replace the eggs with a flaxseed mixture (1 tablespoon ground flaxseed mixed with 3 tablespoons water equals one egg) and use a plant-based cheese alternative.

76. Einkorn Herb and Cheese Biscuits

Number of servings: 12 biscuits

Preparation time: 20 minutes

Cooking time: 15 minutes

Ingredients:

- 2 cups fresh-milled einkorn flour
- 1 tablespoon baking powder
- 1/2 teaspoon salt
- 1/2 cup cold unsalted butter, cubed
- 1 cup shredded sharp cheddar cheese
- 1 tablespoon fresh chopped herbs (such as rosemary, thyme, or chives)
- 3/4 cup whole milk

Directions:

1. Preheat your oven to 425°F (218°C) and line a baking sheet with parchment paper.

2. In a large bowl, whisk together the einkorn flour, baking powder, and salt.

3. Add the cold, cubed butter to the flour mixture. Using a pastry blender or your fingers, cut the butter into the flour until the mixture resembles coarse crumbs.

4. Stir in the shredded cheddar cheese and chopped herbs until evenly distributed.

5. Gradually add the milk, stirring just until the dough comes together. Be careful not to overmix.

6. Turn the dough out onto a lightly floured surface and gently knead it a few times to bring it together.

7. Pat the dough into a 1-inch thick rectangle. Use a biscuit cutter or a glass to cut out biscuits. Re-form the scraps to cut out additional biscuits.

8. Place the biscuits on the prepared baking sheet, leaving about 2 inches between each.

9. Bake in the preheated oven for 15 minutes, or until the biscuits are golden brown on top.

10. Remove from the oven and let cool slightly on the baking sheet before transferring to a wire rack to cool further.

Nutritional value per serving:

- Calories: 220
- Carbs: 18g
- Fiber: 1g
- Sugars: 1g
- Protein: 6g
- Saturated fat: 7g
- Unsaturated fat: 3g

Difficulty rating: Easy

Tips for ingredient variations:

- Substitute the sharp cheddar cheese with any other hard cheese of your choice, such as Gruyère or Parmesan, for a different flavor profile.

- Mix in 1/2 cup of cooked and crumbled bacon or ham to the dough for a savory twist.

- For a lighter version, use low-fat milk and reduced-fat cheese, though the texture may be slightly altered.

77. Einkorn Spicy Bread Twists

Number of servings: 12 twists

Preparation time: 20 minutes

Cooking time: 15 minutes

Ingredients:

- 2 cups fresh-milled einkorn flour
- 1 teaspoon salt
- 1 tablespoon sugar
- 1 tablespoon instant yeast
- 3/4 cup warm water
- 2 tablespoons olive oil
- 1/2 teaspoon garlic powder
- 1/2 teaspoon onion powder
- 1 teaspoon smoked paprika
- 1/4 teaspoon cayenne pepper
- 1 tablespoon melted butter for brushing
- Coarse sea salt for sprinkling

Directions:

1. In a large mixing bowl, combine the fresh-milled einkorn flour, salt, sugar, and instant yeast.

2. Add the warm water and olive oil to the dry ingredients. Mix until a soft dough forms.

3. Turn the dough out onto a lightly floured surface and knead for about 5 minutes, until smooth and elastic.

4. Place the dough in a greased bowl, cover with a damp cloth, and let it rise in a warm place for about 1 hour, or until doubled in size.

5. Preheat your oven to 425°F (220°C) and line a baking sheet with parchment paper.

6. Punch down the dough and turn it out onto a floured surface. Divide the dough into 12 equal pieces.

7. Roll each piece into a long rope, about 12 inches long. Twist each rope into a spiral shape and place on the prepared baking sheet.

8. In a small bowl, mix together the garlic powder, onion powder, smoked paprika, and cayenne pepper. Sprinkle this spice mix over the twisted dough.

9. Brush each twist with melted butter and sprinkle with coarse sea salt.

10. Bake in the preheated oven for 15 minutes, or until golden brown and crispy.

11. Remove from the oven and let cool on a wire rack before serving.

Nutritional value per serving:

- Calories: 150
- Carbs: 24g
- Fiber: 2g
- Sugars: 1g
- Protein: 4g
- Saturated fat: 1g
- Unsaturated fat: 2g

Difficulty rating: Easy

Tips for ingredient variations:

- For a cheesier twist, add 1/2 cup of grated Parmesan cheese to the spice mix before sprinkling on the dough.

- Substitute smoked paprika with chili powder for a different flavor profile.

- For a vegan version, use plant-based butter for brushing.

78. Einkorn Stuffed Mushrooms

Number of servings: 12

Preparation time: 20 minutes

Cooking time: 25 minutes

Ingredients:

- 24 large mushrooms, stems removed and finely chopped
- 2 tablespoons olive oil
- 1/2 cup onion, finely chopped
- 2 cloves garlic, minced
- 1 cup fresh-milled einkorn flour
- 1/2 cup grated Parmesan cheese
- 1/4 cup bread crumbs
- 1/4 cup fresh parsley, chopped
- 1/4 cup chicken or vegetable broth
- Salt and pepper to taste

Directions:

1. Preheat the oven to 375°F (190°C). Grease a baking sheet or line it with parchment paper.

2. In a large skillet over medium heat, heat the olive oil. Add the chopped mushroom stems, onion, and garlic. Cook until the vegetables are softened, about 5-7 minutes.

3. Remove the skillet from heat. Stir in the fresh-milled einkorn flour, Parmesan cheese, bread crumbs, and parsley until well combined. Gradually add the broth, stirring until the mixture is moistened. Season with salt and pepper.

4. Spoon the filling into each mushroom cap, pressing down gently to pack the filling.

5. Arrange the stuffed mushrooms on the prepared baking sheet.

6. Bake in the preheated oven for 20-25 minutes, or until the mushrooms are tender and the tops are golden brown.

7. Serve warm.

Nutritional value per serving: Calories: 120, Carbs: 12g, Fiber: 2g, Sugars: 1g, Protein: 5g, Saturated fat: 2g, Unsaturated fat: 3g

Difficulty rating: Medium

Tips for ingredient variations:

- For a gluten-free version, substitute fresh-milled einkorn flour with almond flour or any gluten-free flour blend.

- Add 1/2 cup of finely chopped cooked sausage or bacon to the filling for a meaty version.

- For a vegan option, omit the Parmesan cheese and use nutritional yeast instead, and replace the broth with vegetable broth.

79. Einkorn Vegetable Empanadas

Number of servings: 8

Preparation time: 45 minutes

Cooking time: 25 minutes

Ingredients:

- For the dough:
  - 2 cups fresh-milled einkorn flour
  - 1/4 cup unsalted butter, chilled
  - 1/2 teaspoon salt
  - 6-8 tablespoons ice water
- For the filling:
  - 1 tablespoon olive oil
  - 1 small onion, finely chopped
  - 1 clove garlic, minced
  - 1 cup spinach, chopped
  - 1/2 cup corn kernels
  - 1/2 cup black beans, rinsed and drained
  - 1/2 cup diced bell peppers
  - 1 teaspoon ground cumin
  - Salt and pepper to taste
- 1 egg, beaten (for egg wash)

Directions:

1. In a large bowl, combine einkorn flour and salt. Cut in the butter until the mixture resembles coarse crumbs. Gradually add ice water, stirring until the dough comes together. Form into a disk, wrap in plastic, and chill for 30 minutes.

2. Heat olive oil in a skillet over medium heat. Add onion and garlic, cooking until softened. Stir in spinach, corn, black beans, bell peppers, and cumin. Cook for 5 minutes, or until vegetables are tender. Season with salt and pepper. Let the filling cool.

3. Preheat the oven to 375°F (190°C). Line a baking sheet with parchment paper.

4. On a floured surface, roll out the dough to 1/8-inch thickness. Cut into 8 circles, about 5 inches in diameter.

5. Spoon the filling onto one half of each circle, leaving a border. Brush the edges with water, fold the dough over the filling to create a half-moon shape, and press the edges to seal.

6. Place the empanadas on the prepared baking sheet. Brush the tops with beaten egg.

7. Bake for 25 minutes, or until golden brown. Let cool slightly before serving.

Nutritional value per serving: Calories: 220, Carbs: 30g, Fiber: 4g, Sugars: 2g, Protein: 5g, Saturated fat: 3g, Unsaturated fat: 2g

Difficulty rating: Medium

Tips for ingredient variations:

- Substitute spinach with kale or Swiss chard for a different flavor profile.

- Add cooked, shredded chicken or ground beef for a protein-packed version.

- For a spicier empanada, include diced jalapeños in the filling or serve with a side of hot sauce.

80. Einkorn Savory Scones

Number of servings: 8 scones

Preparation time: 20 minutes

Cooking time: 22 minutes

Ingredients:

- 2 cups fresh-milled einkorn flour
- 1 tablespoon baking powder
- 1/2 teaspoon salt
- 1/4 teaspoon black pepper
- 1/2 cup cold unsalted butter, cut into small pieces
- 3/4 cup heavy cream, plus more for brushing
- 1 large egg
- 1/2 cup grated sharp cheddar cheese
- 1/4 cup finely chopped fresh chives
- 1/4 cup diced cooked bacon (about 3 slices)

Directions:

1. Preheat the oven to 400°F (200°C). Line a baking sheet with parchment paper.
2. In a large bowl, whisk together the einkorn flour, baking powder, salt, and black pepper.
3. Add the cold butter pieces to the flour mixture. Using a pastry blender or your fingers, cut the butter into the flour until the mixture resembles coarse crumbs.
4. In a small bowl, whisk together the heavy cream and egg. Pour this into the flour mixture, stirring just until the dough starts to come together.
5. Gently fold in the cheddar cheese, chives, and cooked bacon, being careful not to overmix.
6. Turn the dough out onto a lightly floured surface and knead gently just until it comes together. Pat the dough into a circle about 1 inch thick.
7. Using a sharp knife, cut the dough into 8 wedges. Place the wedges on the prepared baking sheet, leaving a few inches between each.
8. Brush the tops of the scones with a little extra heavy cream.
9. Bake for 20-22 minutes, or until the scones are golden brown and a toothpick inserted into the center comes out clean.
10. Remove from the oven and let cool on the baking sheet for 5 minutes, then transfer to a wire rack to cool completely.

Nutritional value per serving:

- Calories: 320
- Carbs: 25g
- Fiber: 1g
- Sugars: 1g
- Protein: 7g
- Saturated fat: 15g
- Unsaturated fat: 5g

Difficulty rating: Medium

Tips for ingredient variations:

- Substitute the cheddar cheese with any other hard cheese of your choice, such as Gruyère or Parmesan, for a different flavor.
- For a vegetarian version, omit the bacon and add an additional 1/4 cup of your favorite vegetables, such as diced bell peppers or sun-dried tomatoes.
- Add a pinch of cayenne pepper to the dough for a spicy kick.

Chapter 6: Pasta and Noodle Recipes

81. Einkorn Spaghetti with Garlic and Olive Oil

Number of servings: 4

Preparation time: 10 minutes

Cooking time: 15 minutes

Ingredients:

- 8 ounces einkorn spaghetti
- 4 tablespoons extra virgin olive oil
- 4 cloves garlic, thinly sliced
- 1/4 teaspoon red pepper flakes (optional)
- Salt, to taste
- Freshly ground black pepper, to taste
- 1/4 cup fresh parsley, chopped
- Grated Parmesan cheese, for serving

Directions:

1. Bring a large pot of salted water to a boil. Add the einkorn spaghetti and cook according to the package instructions until al dente. Drain, reserving 1 cup of pasta water, and set aside.

2. While the pasta is cooking, heat the olive oil in a large skillet over medium heat. Add the sliced garlic and red pepper flakes if using. Cook, stirring frequently, until the garlic is golden brown, about 2 minutes.

3. Add the cooked spaghetti to the skillet. Toss well to coat the spaghetti in the garlic oil. If the pasta seems dry, add a little of the reserved pasta water until it reaches your desired consistency.

4. Season with salt and freshly ground black pepper to taste. Stir in the chopped parsley.

5. Serve immediately, topped with grated Parmesan cheese.

Nutritional value per serving:

- Calories: 380
- Carbs: 56g
- Fiber: 2g
- Sugars: 1g
- Protein: 10g
- Saturated fat: 3g
- Unsaturated fat: 10g

Difficulty rating: Easy

Tips for ingredient variations:

- For an added protein boost, toss in cooked shrimp or chicken with the garlic.

- Substitute parsley with basil for a different herbaceous note.

- Add a squeeze of lemon juice before serving for a fresh citrusy zing.

- For a heartier dish, incorporate sautéed mushrooms or cherry tomatoes along with the garlic.

82. Einkorn Fettuccine Alfredo

Number of servings: 4

Preparation time: 15 minutes

Cooking time: 20 minutes

Ingredients:

- 8 ounces fresh-milled einkorn fettuccine
- 1 cup heavy cream
- 1/2 cup unsalted butter
- 1 cup freshly grated Parmesan cheese
- Salt and pepper to taste
- Fresh parsley, chopped (for garnish)

Directions:

1. Bring a large pot of salted water to a boil. Add the einkorn fettuccine and cook according to package instructions, until al dente. Drain and set aside.

2. In a large skillet over medium heat, combine the heavy cream and butter. Cook, stirring constantly, until the butter is melted and the cream is heated through.

3. Reduce the heat to low and gradually stir in the grated Parmesan cheese until the sauce is smooth and creamy. Season with salt and pepper.

4. Add the cooked fettuccine to the sauce, tossing gently to coat the pasta evenly.

5. Serve immediately, garnished with chopped parsley.

Nutritional value per serving:

- Calories: 650
- Carbs: 47g
- Fiber: 2g
- Sugars: 2g
- Protein: 20g
- Saturated fat: 30g
- Unsaturated fat: 15g

Difficulty rating: Easy

Tips for ingredient variations:

- For a lighter version, substitute half of the heavy cream with whole milk.
- Add sautéed mushrooms or cooked chicken strips to the sauce for added protein.
- Sprinkle crushed red pepper flakes into the sauce for a spicy kick.

83. Einkorn Linguine with Clam Sauce

Number of servings: 4

Preparation time: 20 minutes

Cooking time: 15 minutes

Ingredients:

- 8 ounces einkorn linguine
- 2 tablespoons olive oil
- 4 cloves garlic, minced
- 1/2 teaspoon red pepper flakes
- 2 cans (6.5 ounces each) chopped clams, drained, juice reserved
- 1/2 cup dry white wine
- 1/2 cup fresh parsley, chopped
- Salt and black pepper to taste
- Grated Parmesan cheese, for serving
- Lemon wedges, for serving

Directions:

1. Cook the einkorn linguine according to package instructions in a large pot of salted boiling water until al dente. Drain and set aside.

2. In a large skillet, heat the olive oil over medium heat. Add the minced garlic and red pepper flakes, sautéing for 1 minute until fragrant.

3. Stir in the reserved clam juice and white wine. Bring to a simmer and let cook for 5 minutes to reduce slightly.

4. Add the chopped clams to the skillet and cook for an additional 2-3 minutes, until the clams are heated through.

5. Toss the cooked linguine with the clam sauce in the skillet. Add the chopped parsley and season with salt and black pepper to taste.

6. Serve the linguine with grated Parmesan cheese and lemon wedges on the side.

Nutritional value per serving:

- Calories: 380
- Carbs: 56g
- Fiber: 2g
- Sugars: 2g
- Protein: 18g
- Saturated fat: 2g
- Unsaturated fat: 5g

Difficulty rating: Easy

Tips for ingredient variations:

- For a gluten-free version, substitute einkorn linguine with your favorite gluten-free pasta.

- Add a splash of heavy cream to the sauce for a richer, creamier version.

- Incorporate fresh cherry tomatoes in the sauce for a burst of sweetness.

- Replace clams with shrimp or scallops for a different seafood option.

84. Einkorn Pesto Pasta

Number of servings: 4

Preparation time: 15 minutes

Cooking time: 10 minutes

Ingredients:

- 8 ounces fresh-milled einkorn spaghetti
- 2 cups fresh basil leaves
- 1/3 cup pine nuts
- 2 garlic cloves, peeled
- 1/2 cup grated Parmesan cheese
- 1/2 cup extra-virgin olive oil
- Salt and pepper to taste

Directions:

1. Bring a large pot of salted water to a boil. Add the einkorn spaghetti and cook according to package instructions until al dente. Drain and set aside, reserving 1 cup of pasta water.

2. In a food processor, combine the basil leaves, pine nuts, and garlic cloves. Pulse until coarsely chopped.

3. Add the grated Parmesan cheese to the food processor. With the processor running, gradually pour in the olive oil until the mixture is smooth. Season with salt and pepper to taste.

4. In a large bowl, toss the cooked einkorn spaghetti with the pesto sauce, adding reserved pasta water a little at a time as needed to moisten.

5. Serve immediately, garnished with additional Parmesan cheese if desired.

Nutritional value per serving:

- Calories: 580
- Carbs: 47g
- Fiber: 6g
- Sugars: 2g
- Protein: 16g
- Saturated fat: 6g
- Unsaturated fat: 18g

Difficulty rating: Easy

Tips for ingredient variations:

- Substitute pine nuts with walnuts or almonds for a different nutty flavor.

- Add 1/2 cup of sun-dried tomatoes or roasted red peppers to the pesto for a sweet and tangy twist.

- For a vegan version, replace the Parmesan cheese with nutritional yeast or a vegan Parmesan alternative.

85. Einkorn Lasagna

Number of servings: 8

Preparation time: 1 hour

Cooking time: 45 minutes

Ingredients:

- 9 lasagna noodles, fresh-milled einkorn flour based
- 2 tablespoons olive oil
- 1 large onion, chopped
- 2 garlic cloves, minced
- 1 pound ground beef
- 1 (28 ounces) can crushed tomatoes
- 2 tablespoons tomato paste
- 1/2 cup water
- 1 teaspoon salt
- 1/2 teaspoon ground black pepper
- 1 teaspoon dried basil leaves
- 1 teaspoon dried oregano leaves
- 15 ounces ricotta cheese
- 1 egg
- 3 cups shredded mozzarella cheese
- 1 cup grated Parmesan cheese

Directions:

1. Preheat the oven to 375°F (190°C).
2. Cook the einkorn lasagna noodles according to package instructions; set aside.
3. In a large skillet, heat olive oil over medium heat. Add onion and garlic, sauté until softened, about 5 minutes.
4. Add ground beef to the skillet and cook until browned. Drain excess fat.
5. Stir in crushed tomatoes, tomato paste, water, salt, pepper, basil, and oregano. Bring to a simmer and cook for 15 minutes.
6. In a bowl, mix ricotta cheese, egg, 2 cups of mozzarella cheese, and 1/2 cup of Parmesan cheese.
7. Spread 1 cup of meat sauce in the bottom of a 9x13 inch baking dish. Layer with 3 lasagna noodles, 1/3 of the ricotta cheese mixture, and 1 cup of meat sauce. Repeat layers twice.
8. Top with remaining mozzarella and Parmesan cheese.
9. Cover with foil and bake for 25 minutes. Remove foil and bake for an additional 20 minutes, or until cheese is golden and bubbly.
10. Let stand for 10 minutes before serving.

Nutritional value per serving:

- Calories: 560
- Carbs: 38g
- Fiber: 3g
- Sugars: 5g
- Protein: 35g
- Saturated fat: 18g
- Unsaturated fat: 10g

Difficulty rating: Medium

Tips for ingredient variations:

- For a vegetarian version, substitute ground beef with a mix of mushrooms, zucchini, and spinach. Cook vegetables with onions and garlic before adding to the tomato sauce.

- Add a layer of sliced zucchini or eggplant between the noodles and cheese mixture for extra vegetables.

- Substitute ricotta cheese with cottage cheese for a different texture and flavor in the cheese mixture.

86. Einkorn Macaroni and Cheese

Number of servings: 6

Preparation time: 20 minutes

Cooking time: 20 minutes

Ingredients:

- 2 cups fresh-milled einkorn flour
- 1 tablespoon olive oil
- 1 teaspoon salt
- 4 cups water (for boiling pasta)
- 2 cups sharp cheddar cheese, grated
- 1 cup whole milk
- 1/2 cup unsalted butter
- 1/4 cup all-purpose flour
- 1/2 teaspoon paprika
- 1/4 teaspoon black pepper
- 1/2 teaspoon garlic powder
- 1/2 cup breadcrumbs

Directions:

1. In a large pot, bring 4 cups of water to a boil. Add 1 teaspoon salt and 1 tablespoon olive oil.

2. Gradually stir in 2 cups of fresh-milled einkorn flour to make the pasta dough. Knead until smooth, then roll out and cut into macaroni shapes. Add the pasta to boiling water and cook for 8 minutes or until al dente. Drain and set aside.

3. In a separate saucepan, melt the butter over medium heat. Whisk in the all-purpose flour until smooth to create a roux. Cook for 2 minutes, stirring constantly.

4. Gradually add the milk to the roux, stirring constantly until the mixture thickens.

5. Reduce the heat to low and add the grated cheddar cheese, paprika, black pepper, and garlic powder. Stir until the cheese is melted and the sauce is smooth.

6. Combine the cooked pasta and cheese sauce in a large bowl, stirring until the pasta is evenly coated.

7. Transfer the macaroni and cheese to a greased baking dish. Sprinkle breadcrumbs over the top.

8. Bake in a preheated oven at 350°F (175°C) for 10 minutes or until the breadcrumbs are golden brown.

9. Serve warm.

Nutritional value per serving:

- Calories: 520
- Carbs: 48g
- Fiber: 2g
- Sugars: 3g
- Protein: 18g
- Saturated fat: 20g
- Unsaturated fat: 10g

Difficulty rating: Medium

Tips for ingredient variations:

- For a gluten-free version, substitute all-purpose flour with a gluten-free flour blend for the roux and use gluten-free breadcrumbs.

- Add cooked bacon, ham, or broccoli for extra flavor and texture.

- For a spicier version, add 1/2 teaspoon of cayenne pepper to the cheese sauce.

87. Einkorn Pad Thai

Number of servings: 4

Preparation time: 30 minutes

Cooking time: 15 minutes

Ingredients:

- 8 ounces fresh-milled einkorn spaghetti
- 2 tablespoons olive oil
- 2 cloves garlic, minced
- 1/2 pound shrimp, peeled and deveined
- 2 eggs
- 1/4 cup fresh lime juice
- 2 tablespoons fish sauce
- 1 tablespoon sugar
- 1/2 teaspoon red pepper flakes
- 1 cup bean sprouts
- 1/4 cup crushed peanuts
- 1/4 cup chopped fresh cilantro
- 1/4 cup sliced green onions
- Lime wedges for serving

Directions:

1. Cook the einkorn spaghetti according to package instructions until al dente. Drain and set aside.

2. Heat olive oil in a large skillet over medium heat. Add garlic and shrimp, cooking until the shrimp are pink and opaque, about 3-4 minutes. Remove shrimp from the skillet and set aside.

3. In a small bowl, whisk together the eggs, lime juice, fish sauce, sugar, and red pepper flakes.

4. In the same skillet used for the shrimp, pour in the egg mixture, stirring constantly until the eggs begin to set but are still moist, about 2 minutes.

5. Add the cooked spaghetti to the skillet, tossing to combine with the egg mixture. Cook for an additional 2 minutes.

6. Return the shrimp to the skillet, add bean sprouts, and toss everything together until well mixed and heated through, about 2 more minutes.

7. Serve the pad Thai sprinkled with crushed peanuts, cilantro, green onions, and lime wedges on the side.

Nutritional value per serving:

- Calories: 450
- Carbs: 58g
- Fiber: 6g
- Sugars: 5g
- Protein: 25g
- Saturated fat: 2g
- Unsaturated fat: 5g

Difficulty rating: Medium

Tips for ingredient variations:

- For a vegetarian version, omit the shrimp and add tofu or additional vegetables such as bell peppers or zucchini.

- Adjust the level of spiciness by increasing or decreasing the amount of red pepper flakes.

- Substitute chicken or beef for the shrimp if desired.

88. Einkorn Ramen Noodle Soup

Number of servings: 4

Preparation time: 20 minutes

Cooking time: 30 minutes

Ingredients:

- For the Ramen Noodles:
  - 2 cups fresh-milled einkorn flour
  - 1/2 teaspoon salt
  - 2 large eggs
  - 3 tablespoons water
- For the Soup:
  - 4 cups chicken or vegetable broth
  - 2 cups water
  - 1 tablespoon soy sauce
  - 1 tablespoon miso paste
  - 2 cloves garlic, minced
  - 1 inch piece ginger, grated
  - 1/2 cup sliced mushrooms
  - 1/2 cup chopped green onions
  - 1 cup shredded cooked chicken or tofu (optional)
  - 2 boiled eggs, halved
  - 1/2 cup fresh spinach leaves

Directions:

1. Start by making the ramen noodles. In a large bowl, mix together the einkorn flour and salt. Make a well in the center and add the eggs and water. Gradually incorporate the flour into the eggs and water, kneading until a smooth dough forms. If the dough is too dry, add a little more water, one teaspoon at a time.

2. Roll the dough out on a floured surface until it is very thin. Cut the dough into thin strips to resemble ramen noodles. Set aside.

3. In a large pot, bring the chicken or vegetable broth and water to a boil. Lower the heat to medium and add the soy sauce, miso paste, garlic, and ginger. Stir until the miso paste is fully dissolved.

4. Add the sliced mushrooms and green onions to the pot. Simmer for 5 minutes.

5. Bring the soup back to a boil and add the freshly made einkorn ramen noodles. Cook for 3-4 minutes, or until the noodles are tender.

6. If using, add the shredded cooked chicken or tofu and spinach leaves, and cook for an additional 2 minutes, or until the spinach is wilted and the chicken or tofu is heated through.

7. Serve the soup hot, garnished with boiled egg halves.

Nutritional value per serving:

- Calories: 350
- Carbs: 45g
- Fiber: 3g
- Sugars: 2g
- Protein: 20g
- Saturated fat: 3g
- Unsaturated fat: 2g

Difficulty rating: Medium

Tips for ingredient variations:

- For a vegetarian version, use vegetable broth and tofu instead of chicken.

- Add other vegetables like bok choy, carrots, or bell peppers to the soup for extra nutrition and flavor.

- For a gluten-free option, substitute einkorn flour with your preferred gluten-free flour blend for the noodles, adjusting the liquid as needed to achieve the right dough consistency.

89. Einkorn Udon Noodles with Soy Sauce

Number of servings: 4

Preparation time: 1 hour

Cooking time: 10 minutes

Ingredients:

- For the noodles:
  - 2 cups fresh-milled einkorn flour
  - 3/4 cup warm water
  - 1/2 teaspoon salt
- For the soy sauce mixture:
  - 1/4 cup soy sauce
  - 2 tablespoons mirin
  - 1 tablespoon sugar
  - 1 clove garlic, minced
  - 1 teaspoon grated fresh ginger
  - 2 tablespoons water
- Optional toppings:
  - Sliced green onions
  - Sesame seeds
  - Sliced chili peppers

Directions:

1. In a large mixing bowl, combine the fresh-milled einkorn flour and salt. Gradually add warm water, stirring until a dough forms.

2. Knead the dough on a lightly floured surface for about 10 minutes, until smooth and elastic. Cover with a damp cloth and let rest for 30 minutes.

3. Roll out the dough on a floured surface to about 1/8-inch thickness. Fold the dough in layers, then cut into thin strips to form noodles.

4. Bring a large pot of water to a boil. Cook the noodles for about 5-7 minutes, or until tender. Drain and rinse under cold water to stop the cooking process.

5. In a small saucepan, combine soy sauce, mirin, sugar, garlic, ginger, and water. Bring to a simmer over medium heat, stirring until the sugar dissolves. Remove from heat.

6. Toss the cooked noodles with the soy sauce mixture until evenly coated.

7. Serve the noodles in bowls, garnished with optional toppings of sliced green onions, sesame seeds, and sliced chili peppers.

Nutritional value per serving:

- Calories: 310
- Carbs: 58g
- Fiber: 8g
- Sugars: 6g
- Protein: 9g
- Saturated fat: 0g
- Unsaturated fat: 1g

Difficulty rating: Medium

Tips for ingredient variations:

- For a gluten-free version, substitute einkorn flour with your preferred gluten-free flour blend, adjusting the water amount if necessary.

- Add sliced cooked chicken, shrimp, or tofu to the noodles for added protein.

- Incorporate stir-fried vegetables such as bell peppers, broccoli, or mushrooms for a more nutritious and filling meal.

90. Einkorn Penne Arrabbiata

Number of servings: 4

Preparation time: 20 minutes

Cooking time: 20 minutes

Ingredients:

- 8 ounces einkorn penne pasta
- 2 tablespoons olive oil
- 4 garlic cloves, minced
- 1/2 teaspoon red pepper flakes
- 1 can (28 ounces) crushed tomatoes
- Salt to taste
- 1/4 cup fresh basil leaves, chopped
- Grated Parmesan cheese, for serving

Directions:

1. Bring a large pot of salted water to a boil. Add the einkorn penne pasta and cook according to package instructions until al dente. Drain and set aside.

2. In a large skillet, heat the olive oil over medium heat. Add the minced garlic and red pepper flakes, sautéing for about 1 minute until fragrant.

3. Stir in the crushed tomatoes and a pinch of salt. Bring to a simmer and cook for 10 minutes, stirring occasionally.

4. Add the cooked einkorn penne to the sauce, tossing to coat evenly. Cook for an additional 2 minutes to allow the pasta to absorb some of the sauce.

5. Remove from heat and stir in the chopped fresh basil.

6. Serve hot, garnished with grated Parmesan cheese.

Nutritional value per serving:

- Calories: 350
- Carbs: 58g
- Fiber: 6g
- Sugars: 8g
- Protein: 10g
- Saturated fat: 2g
- Unsaturated fat: 5g

Difficulty rating: Easy

Tips for ingredient variations:

- For a protein boost, add cooked chicken breast or shrimp to the sauce during the last 5 minutes of cooking.

- Substitute crushed tomatoes with fresh cherry tomatoes halved, cooked down until soft and saucy.

- For extra vegetables, stir in spinach or kale during the last few minutes of cooking the sauce.

91. Einkorn Sesame Noodles

Number of servings: 4

Preparation time: 20 minutes

Cooking time: 10 minutes

Ingredients:

- 8 ounces fresh-milled einkorn spaghetti or noodles
- 2 tablespoons sesame oil
- 3 tablespoons soy sauce
- 1 tablespoon rice vinegar
- 2 teaspoons honey or maple syrup
- 1 tablespoon grated fresh ginger
- 2 cloves garlic, minced
- 2 tablespoons toasted sesame seeds
- 1/4 cup thinly sliced green onions
- 1/4 cup chopped cilantro (optional)
- Red pepper flakes to taste (optional)

Directions:

1. Cook the einkorn spaghetti or noodles according to package instructions until al dente. Drain and rinse under cold water to stop the cooking process. Set aside.

2. In a large bowl, whisk together sesame oil, soy sauce, rice vinegar, honey or maple syrup, grated ginger, and minced garlic to create the sauce.

3. Add the cooked noodles to the sauce in the bowl. Toss until the noodles are evenly coated.

4. Stir in the toasted sesame seeds, sliced green onions, and chopped cilantro (if using). Add red pepper flakes to taste, if desired.

5. Serve the noodles chilled or at room temperature, garnished with additional sesame seeds and green onions.

Nutritional value per serving:

- Calories: 320
- Carbs: 45g
- Fiber: 3g
- Sugars: 5g
- Protein: 8g
- Saturated fat: 1g
- Unsaturated fat: 5g

Difficulty rating: Easy

Tips for ingredient variations:

- For a gluten-free version, ensure the soy sauce is gluten-free or substitute with tamari.

- Add shredded cooked chicken, tofu, or shrimp for added protein.

- Incorporate julienned vegetables such as carrots, bell peppers, or cucumber for a refreshing crunch and nutritional boost.

92. Einkorn Carbonara

Number of servings: 4

Preparation time: 20 minutes

Cooking time: 15 minutes

Ingredients:

- 8 ounces einkorn spaghetti
- 4 large eggs
- 1 cup freshly grated Parmesan cheese
- 8 slices bacon, chopped
- 2 cloves garlic, minced
- Salt and black pepper to taste
- Fresh parsley, chopped (for garnish)

Directions:

1. Cook the einkorn spaghetti according to package instructions in a large pot of salted boiling water until al dente. Drain, reserving 1/2 cup of the pasta water, and set aside.

2. While the pasta is cooking, whisk together the eggs and Parmesan cheese in a bowl until well combined. Set aside.

3. In a large skillet over medium heat, cook the bacon until crisp. Add the minced garlic to the bacon and cook for an additional minute until fragrant.

4. Add the cooked spaghetti to the skillet with the bacon and garlic. Toss to combine and remove from heat.

5. Quickly pour the egg and cheese mixture over the spaghetti, tossing continuously with tongs to coat the pasta and prevent the eggs from scrambling. If the sauce is too thick, add a little of the reserved pasta water until it reaches your desired consistency.

6. Season with salt and black pepper to taste. Serve immediately, garnished with chopped parsley and additional grated Parmesan cheese if desired.

Nutritional value per serving:

- Calories: 520
- Carbs: 48g
- Fiber: 2g
- Sugars: 2g
- Protein: 25g
- Saturated fat: 10g
- Unsaturated fat: 15g

Difficulty rating: Medium

Tips for ingredient variations:

- For a lighter version, substitute the bacon with turkey bacon or omit it entirely for a vegetarian option.

- Add sautéed mushrooms or spinach to the pasta before adding the egg mixture for extra vegetables.

- For a spicy kick, add a pinch of red pepper flakes to the bacon and garlic while cooking.

93. Einkorn Gnocchi with Marinara Sauce

Number of servings: 4

Preparation time: 1 hour

Cooking time: 3 minutes

Ingredients:

- **For the Gnocchi**:
  - 2 cups fresh-milled einkorn flour
  - 1 pound russet potatoes (about 2 medium-sized), baked and cooled
  - 1 large egg, lightly beaten
  - 1/2 teaspoon salt
- **For the Marinara Sauce**:
  - 2 tablespoons olive oil
  - 1 small onion, finely chopped
  - 2 garlic cloves, minced
  - 1 can (28 ounces) crushed tomatoes
  - 1 teaspoon dried basil
  - 1 teaspoon dried oregano
  - Salt and pepper to taste
  - Fresh basil leaves, for garnish

Directions:

1. Start by making the gnocchi. Peel the baked potatoes and pass them through a potato ricer into a large bowl.

2. Add the fresh-milled einkorn flour, egg, and salt to the riced potatoes. Gently mix until a soft dough forms. Be careful not to overwork the dough.

3. On a floured surface, divide the dough into four equal parts. Roll each part into a long rope, about 1/2 inch in diameter. Cut the ropes into 1-inch pieces.

4. Bring a large pot of salted water to a boil. Cook the gnocchi in batches, dropping them into the boiling water. They are done when they float to the surface, about 2-3 minutes. Remove with a slotted spoon and set aside.

5. For the marinara sauce, heat the olive oil in a saucepan over medium heat. Add the onion and garlic, sautéing until soft and translucent, about 5 minutes.

6. Add the crushed tomatoes, basil, oregano, salt, and pepper. Simmer for 20 minutes, stirring occasionally.

7. To serve, divide the gnocchi among plates and top with the marinara sauce. Garnish with fresh basil leaves.

Nutritional value per serving:

- Calories: 380
- Carbs: 65g
- Fiber: 5g
- Sugars: 6g
- Protein: 10g
- Saturated fat: 2g
- Unsaturated fat: 5g

Difficulty rating: Medium

Tips for ingredient variations:

- For a richer gnocchi, add 1/4 cup grated Parmesan cheese to the dough.

- Incorporate spinach into the marinara sauce for added nutrients by adding 1 cup of fresh spinach leaves during the last 5 minutes of simmering.

- For a spicy marinara sauce, add 1/2 teaspoon of red pepper flakes along with the tomatoes.

94. Einkorn Ravioli with Spinach and Ricotta

Number of servings: 4

Preparation time: 1 hour

Cooking time: 25 minutes

Ingredients:

- For the dough:
  - 2 cups fresh-milled einkorn flour
  - 3 large eggs
  - 1/2 teaspoon salt
- For the filling:
  - 1 cup ricotta cheese
  - 1 cup fresh spinach, finely chopped
  - 1/2 cup grated Parmesan cheese
  - 1 egg, beaten
  - Salt and pepper to taste
- Additional flour for dusting
- Salted water for boiling

Directions:

1. In a large mixing bowl, combine 2 cups of fresh-milled einkorn flour with 1/2 teaspoon salt. Make a well in the center and add 3 eggs. Gradually incorporate the flour into the eggs using a fork, working from the center outwards, until a dough forms.

2. Knead the dough on a floured surface for about 10 minutes, until smooth and elastic. Wrap in plastic wrap and let rest for 30 minutes.

3. For the filling, mix together ricotta cheese, chopped spinach, grated Parmesan cheese, 1 beaten egg, and season with salt and pepper in a bowl.

4. After the dough has rested, divide it into four equal portions. Roll out one portion at a time on a floured surface to about 1/16 inch thickness.

5. Place teaspoonfuls of filling about 1 inch apart over half of the rolled-out dough. Fold the other half over the filling. Press around each mound of filling to seal, then cut into individual ravioli with a pastry cutter or knife.

6. Bring a large pot of salted water to a boil. Cook the ravioli in batches for about 4 minutes, or until they float to the surface and are tender.

7. Remove with a slotted spoon and serve with your choice of sauce.

Nutritional value per serving:

- Calories: 450
- Carbs: 45g
- Fiber: 3g
- Sugars: 2g
- Protein: 25g
- Saturated fat: 8g
- Unsaturated fat: 5g

Difficulty rating: Medium

Tips for ingredient variations:

- Substitute spinach with kale or Swiss chard for a different green in the filling.

- Add a pinch of nutmeg to the filling for an aromatic flavor.

- For a vegan version, use a vegan ricotta substitute and omit the egg in the filling, adding a tablespoon of olive oil for moisture if needed.

95. Einkorn Lo Mein

Number of servings: 4

Preparation time: 20 minutes

Cooking time: 15 minutes

Ingredients:

- 8 ounces fresh-milled einkorn spaghetti
- 2 tablespoons olive oil
- 2 garlic cloves, minced
- 1/2 cup low-sodium soy sauce
- 2 tablespoons brown sugar
- 1 tablespoon oyster sauce
- 1 teaspoon sesame oil
- 1 cup mixed vegetables (carrot, bell pepper, snap peas), julienned
- 2 green onions, thinly sliced
- 1 tablespoon sesame seeds

Directions:

1. Cook the einkorn spaghetti according to package instructions until al dente. Drain and set aside.

2. In a large skillet or wok, heat the olive oil over medium heat. Add the minced garlic and sauté for 1 minute until fragrant.

3. In a small bowl, whisk together the soy sauce, brown sugar, oyster sauce, and sesame oil. Pour this mixture into the skillet with the garlic and bring to a simmer.

4. Add the julienned mixed vegetables to the skillet and cook for 3-4 minutes until they are just tender.

5. Add the cooked einkorn spaghetti to the skillet, tossing well to ensure the noodles are evenly coated with the sauce and mixed with the vegetables.

6. Cook for an additional 2 minutes, allowing the flavors to meld together.

7. Serve the lo mein garnished with sliced green onions and sesame seeds.

Nutritional value per serving:

- Calories: 320
- Carbs: 45g
- Fiber: 3g
- Sugars: 8g
- Protein: 9g
- Saturated fat: 1g
- Unsaturated fat: 4g

Difficulty rating: Easy

Tips for ingredient variations:

- For a protein boost, add sliced cooked chicken, beef, or tofu to the lo mein when adding the vegetables.

- Swap out the mixed vegetables for any of your favorites or whatever you have on hand, such as broccoli, mushrooms, or cabbage.

- For a gluten-free version, ensure the soy sauce and oyster sauce are gluten-free and substitute einkorn spaghetti with a gluten-free noodle option.

96. Einkorn Ziti with Sausage and Peppers

Number of servings: 4

Preparation time: 30 minutes

Cooking time: 20 minutes

Ingredients:

- 8 ounces ziti pasta, made from fresh-milled einkorn flour
- 1 tablespoon olive oil
- 1 pound Italian sausage, casing removed
- 1 red bell pepper, sliced
- 1 green bell pepper, sliced
- 1 onion, sliced
- 2 cloves garlic, minced
- 1 can (28 ounces) crushed tomatoes
- 1 teaspoon dried oregano
- 1 teaspoon dried basil
- Salt and pepper to taste
- 1/2 cup grated Parmesan cheese
- Fresh basil leaves for garnish

Directions:

1. Cook the ziti pasta in a large pot of boiling salted water according to package instructions until al dente. Drain and set aside.

2. In a large skillet, heat the olive oil over medium heat. Add the Italian sausage and cook, breaking it apart with a spoon, until browned and cooked through, about 5-7 minutes.

3. Add the sliced bell peppers and onion to the skillet with the sausage. Cook, stirring occasionally, until the vegetables are softened, about 5 minutes.

4. Stir in the minced garlic and cook for an additional minute until fragrant.

5. Add the crushed tomatoes, dried oregano, dried basil, salt, and pepper to the skillet. Simmer the sauce for 10 minutes, allowing the flavors to meld.

6. Toss the cooked ziti pasta with the sausage and pepper sauce until well combined.

7. Serve the ziti garnished with grated Parmesan cheese and fresh basil leaves.

Nutritional value per serving:

- Calories: 650
- Carbs: 58g
- Fiber: 4g
- Sugars: 8g
- Protein: 28g
- Saturated fat: 12g
- Unsaturated fat: 10g

Difficulty rating: Medium

Tips for ingredient variations:

- For a spicier dish, use hot Italian sausage or add red pepper flakes to the sauce.

- Substitute the Italian sausage with ground turkey or chicken for a lighter version.

- Add other vegetables such as mushrooms or spinach to the sauce for extra nutrition.

- For a dairy-free option, omit the Parmesan cheese or use a vegan cheese alternative.

97. Einkorn Orzo Salad

Number of servings: 6

Preparation time: 20 minutes

Cooking time: 10 minutes

Ingredients:

- 1 1/2 cups orzo, fresh-milled einkorn flour based
- 2 tablespoons olive oil
- 1/4 cup red onion, finely chopped
- 1 cucumber, diced
- 1 cup cherry tomatoes, halved
- 1/4 cup kalamata olives, pitted and sliced
- 1/4 cup feta cheese, crumbled
- 2 tablespoons fresh parsley, chopped
- 2 tablespoons fresh lemon juice
- 1 garlic clove, minced
- Salt and pepper to taste

Directions:

1. Bring a large pot of salted water to a boil. Add the einkorn orzo and cook according to package instructions until al dente, about 7-9 minutes. Drain and rinse under cold water to stop the cooking process.

2. In a large mixing bowl, combine the cooked orzo with olive oil, red onion, cucumber, cherry tomatoes, kalamata olives, and feta cheese. Toss to combine.

3. In a small bowl, whisk together the fresh parsley, lemon juice, minced garlic, salt, and pepper. Pour this dressing over the orzo salad and toss again until everything is well coated.

4. Refrigerate the salad for at least 10 minutes before serving to allow the flavors to meld.

Nutritional value per serving:

- Calories: 220
- Carbs: 38g
- Fiber: 3g
- Sugars: 3g
- Protein: 6g
- Saturated fat: 2g
- Unsaturated fat: 3g

Difficulty rating: Easy

Tips for ingredient variations:

- For a protein boost, add grilled chicken or shrimp to the salad.
- Substitute feta cheese with goat cheese for a creamier texture.
- Add roasted red peppers or artichoke hearts for additional flavor and texture.
- For a zestier dressing, include the zest of the lemon used for the juice.

98. Einkorn Tortellini Soup

Number of servings: 6

Preparation time: 30 minutes

Cooking time: 25 minutes

Ingredients:

- **For the Tortellini**:
  - 1 1/2 cups fresh-milled einkorn flour
  - 2 large eggs
  - 1/2 teaspoon salt
  - 1 tablespoon water (if needed)
  - 1/2 cup ricotta cheese
  - 1/4 cup grated Parmesan cheese
  - 1 tablespoon chopped fresh basil

- **For the Soup**:
  - 6 cups chicken or vegetable broth
  - 1 cup chopped carrots
  - 1 cup chopped celery
  - 1/2 cup diced onion
  - 2 cloves garlic, minced
  - 1 cup spinach leaves
  - Salt and pepper to taste
  - Fresh basil for garnish

Directions:

1. Start by making the tortellini dough. In a large bowl, mix together the einkorn flour, eggs, and salt. Knead until a smooth dough forms, adding a tablespoon of water if the dough is too dry. Wrap in plastic and let rest for 20 minutes.

2. For the filling, combine ricotta cheese, Parmesan cheese, and chopped basil in a small bowl. Set aside.

3. Roll out the tortellini dough on a floured surface until about 1/16 inch thick. Cut into 2-inch squares.

4. Place a teaspoon of the cheese mixture in the center of each square. Fold the dough over the filling to form a triangle, pressing the edges to seal. Bring the two bottom corners together and press to seal, forming the tortellini shape.

5. Bring the broth to a boil in a large pot. Add carrots, celery, onion, and garlic. Reduce heat and simmer for 10 minutes.

6. Add the tortellini to the soup and cook for an additional 5 minutes, or until they float to the surface and are tender.

7. Stir in spinach leaves and cook until wilted, about 1 minute. Season with salt and pepper.

8. Serve the soup hot, garnished with fresh basil.

Nutritional value per serving:

- Calories: 280
- Carbs: 35g
- Fiber: 3g
- Sugars: 4g
- Protein: 15g
- Saturated fat: 4g
- Unsaturated fat: 2g

Difficulty rating: Medium

Tips for ingredient variations:

- Swap spinach in the filling for chopped cooked mushrooms or cooked and crumbled sausage for a different flavor.

- Use vegetable broth instead of chicken broth for a vegetarian version of the soup.

- Add a pinch of nutmeg to the tortellini filling for an extra layer of flavor.

99. Einkorn Pho

Number of servings: 4

Preparation time: 30 minutes

Cooking time: 20 minutes

Ingredients:

- For the broth:
  - 8 cups beef or vegetable broth
  - 1 large onion, peeled and halved
  - 4 cloves garlic, smashed
  - 1 3-inch piece of ginger, sliced
  - 2 star anise
  - 2 cinnamon sticks
  - 1 tablespoon fish sauce
  - Salt and pepper to taste
- For the pho:
  - 8 ounces fresh-milled einkorn noodles
  - 1/2 pound thinly sliced beef sirloin or tofu for a vegetarian option
  - 2 cups bean sprouts
  - 1 cup fresh basil leaves
  - 1 cup cilantro leaves
  - 2 jalapeños, thinly sliced
  - 2 limes, cut into wedges
  - Hoisin sauce and Sriracha, for serving

Directions:

1. In a large pot, combine the broth, onion, garlic, ginger, star anise, and cinnamon sticks. Bring to a boil, then reduce heat and simmer for 20 minutes to allow the flavors to meld.

2. Strain the broth and return it to the pot. Stir in the fish sauce and season with salt and pepper. Keep hot over low heat.

3. Cook the einkorn noodles according to package instructions, then drain and divide among four serving bowls.

4. Arrange the thinly sliced beef or tofu over the noodles in the bowls.

5. Pour the hot broth over the beef and noodles in each bowl. The heat from the broth will cook the thin beef slices or warm the tofu.

6. Serve the pho with bean sprouts, basil, cilantro, jalapeños, lime wedges, hoisin sauce, and Sriracha on the side, allowing each person to customize their bowl.

Nutritional value per serving:

- Calories: 350
- Carbs: 40g
- Fiber: 3g
- Sugars: 3g
- Protein: 25g
- Saturated fat: 2g
- Unsaturated fat: 5g

Difficulty rating: Medium

Tips for ingredient variations:

- For a gluten-free version, ensure the fish sauce and hoisin sauce are gluten-free and substitute einkorn noodles with rice noodles.

- Add mushrooms, like sliced shiitake or cremini, to the broth for an earthy flavor.

- For a spicier broth, add more slices of jalapeño or a dash of extra Sriracha.

100. Einkorn Chow Mein

Number of servings: 4

Preparation time: 30 minutes

Cooking time: 15 minutes

Ingredients:

- 8 ounces fresh-milled einkorn spaghetti
- 2 tablespoons olive oil
- 2 cloves garlic, minced
- 2 cups mixed vegetables (carrot, bell pepper, and cabbage), julienned
- 1/2 cup mushrooms, sliced
- 1/4 cup soy sauce
- 2 tablespoons oyster sauce (optional)
- 1 tablespoon sesame oil
- 1/2 teaspoon ground black pepper
- 2 green onions, chopped for garnish
- Sesame seeds for garnish

Directions:

1. Cook the einkorn spaghetti according to package instructions until al dente. Drain and set aside.

2. Heat olive oil in a large skillet or wok over medium-high heat. Add the minced garlic and sauté for 30 seconds, or until fragrant.

3. Add the julienned mixed vegetables and mushrooms to the skillet. Stir-fry for 5-7 minutes, or until the vegetables are tender yet crisp.

4. Stir in the soy sauce, oyster sauce (if using), and sesame oil. Mix well to combine.

5. Add the cooked einkorn spaghetti to the skillet. Toss everything together for 2-3 minutes, ensuring the noodles are well coated with the sauce and vegetables are evenly distributed.

6. Season with ground black pepper. Adjust the seasoning if necessary.

7. Serve hot, garnished with chopped green onions and sesame seeds.

Nutritional value per serving:

- Calories: 320
- Carbs: 45g
- Fiber: 4g
- Sugars: 4g
- Protein: 10g
- Saturated fat: 2g
- Unsaturated fat: 5g

Difficulty rating: Medium

Tips for ingredient variations:

- For a protein boost, add cooked chicken, shrimp, or tofu to the chow mein during step 4.

- Replace soy sauce with tamari for a gluten-free option.

- Incorporate additional vegetables like snap peas, broccoli, or bean sprouts for more variety and crunch.

- For a spicier dish, add a drizzle of chili oil or a sprinkle of red pepper flakes before serving.

Chapter 7: Expertise in Dough Handling

Kneading Techniques for Einkorn Dough

Kneading einkorn dough is an important part of making bread. It needs a careful approach because of its special gluten. Unlike regular wheat, einkorn's gluten is more fragile and less stretchy, which means you have to knead it gently to keep the dough from getting damaged. Here's a simple guide to kneading einkorn dough:

1. **Preparation**: Start by making sure your work area is clean. The surface should be free of dirt or moisture to avoid any contamination. Your hands should also be dry to stop the dough from sticking too much. Lightly sprinkle einkorn flour on the kneading surface to keep the dough from sticking too tightly, but don't use too much flour, as that can change how wet the dough is.

2. **Mixing**: In a large bowl, measure and mix your ingredients according to your recipe. Stir until everything comes together into a rough, shaggy mix. Because einkorn flour absorbs water more slowly than regular wheat, it's important to let the mixture rest for a short time. This helps the flour soak up the water better and creates a more even texture before you start kneading.

3. **Autolyse (Optional)**: To make the dough stronger, you can add an autolyse step. Let the mixed dough sit for 20 to 30 minutes before adding salt or starting to knead. This resting time helps the flour fully absorb water and starts developing gluten naturally, without any extra work. The autolyse phase can make the dough easier to handle and improve the texture of the final bread.

4. **Kneading**: Move the dough to your prepared surface. Use a gentle kneading method by folding the dough over itself and pressing down with the heel of your hand to push it forward. Turn the dough 90 degrees and repeat this motion. It's important to be gentle to avoid overworking it, which can harm the delicate gluten structure. Expect the einkorn dough to stay a bit sticky and soft during this process.

5. **Windowpane Test**: After about 5-10 minutes of kneading, check the gluten development with the windowpane test. Stretch a small piece of the dough between your fingers. The aim is to stretch it thin enough so light can shine through without tearing. While einkorn dough may not be as clear as modern wheat doughs, it should still stretch enough to show good gluten development.

6. **Resting**: Shape the kneaded dough into a ball and place it in a bowl lightly coated with oil to stop it from sticking. Cover the bowl with a damp cloth or plastic wrap to keep moisture in and let the dough rise according to your recipe's timing. A longer, cooler rise is good for einkorn dough, as it helps develop flavor and structure.

7. **Shaping**: After the first rise, gently press the dough down to release excess air and shape it as your recipe directs. Be careful when handling the dough to keep its delicate structure intact, and try not to manipulate it too much to avoid disrupting the gluten network.

8. **Final Proof**: Move the shaped dough to a prepared baking dish or sheet. Cover it to keep moisture in and let it rise again until it nearly doubles in size. This second rise is important for getting the dough ready for baking, which helps with the texture of the finished bread.

9. **Baking**: Follow your recipe's baking instructions carefully. Einkorn breads usually need a slightly lower oven temperature and a longer baking time compared to breads made with modern wheat flour. This adjustment helps ensure the bread bakes evenly and has the right texture in the end.

Troubleshooting Dough Disasters

When baking with einkorn flour, experts may face various dough-related challenges that need careful techniques to fix. Here are some strategies for common issues with einkorn dough:

1. **Dough Too Sticky**: Einkorn dough is stickier than dough made with regular wheat flour due to its unique gluten structure, which is less stretchy and more pliable. If your dough is too sticky, don't make the mistake of adding too much flour, as this can make the final product dense and affect its texture. Instead, lightly dust your hands and the work surface with a small amount of flour. Use a dough scraper to handle the dough, which helps reduce direct contact and stickiness. By gently folding and stretching the dough during kneading, you can improve its texture, making it less sticky and easier to work with.

2. **Dough Too Dry**: If the dough is dry or crumbly, it likely hasn't absorbed enough moisture. Einkorn flour absorbs liquid more slowly than other flours, so take your time. After mixing, if the dough still seems dry, add water gradually, one tablespoon at a time. Let the dough rest briefly after each addition so the flour can soak up the moisture. This careful method helps you avoid making the dough too wet, which could lead to other texture issues.

3. **Insufficient Rise**: Einkorn dough tends to rise more slowly than dough made with high-gluten flours, due to its unique gluten properties. If your dough isn't rising as expected, make sure it's in a warm, draft-free spot, as temperature changes can slow down yeast activity. You might need to let the dough rise longer to give the yeast enough time to create gases for leavening. Using a pre-ferment, like a sponge or poolish, can also boost the rise and add more flavor to the bread. This involves mixing flour, water, and a little yeast and letting it ferment before combining it with the main dough.

4. **Overproofing**: Overproofing einkorn dough can cause bread to collapse in the oven due to too much gas and weakened gluten structure. To avoid this, watch the dough closely during its second rise and use the finger indentation test to check readiness. Lightly press the dough with your fingertip; if it slowly springs back but leaves a slight mark, it's ready to bake. If it collapses, it might be overproofed. In that case, gently press out some gas, reshape the dough with minimal handling, and let it proof for a shorter time before baking.

5. **Tough Crust or Dense Crumb**: A tough crust or dense crumb in einkorn bread can happen due to over-kneading or baking at too high a temperature. Because einkorn's gluten is delicate, knead gently and stop when the dough comes together and feels slightly tacky. This helps develop gluten without damaging its structure. For baking, set the oven temperature a bit lower than you would for breads made with modern wheat flour. Also, using a steam bath in the oven at the start of baking can keep the crust soft, allowing the bread to rise properly without forming a hard outer layer too soon.

Common Dough Preparation Mistakes

In the specialized field of baking with fresh-milled einkorn flour, preparing the dough is a key step that affects the quality of the final baked product, whether it's a loaf of bread or light pastries. A common mistake among bakers is not understanding how much water einkorn flour absorbs. Unlike modern wheat, einkorn has a unique and ancient genetic makeup that interacts with water differently, showing a slower absorption rate. This requires careful handling: instead of quickly adding more flour when the dough seems too wet, which could make it dense and dry, it's important to add water slowly. Allowing the dough to rest during this process lets the einkorn flour fully absorb the water. This step is vital for creating dough that has the right consistency and keeps the hydration levels balanced.

Another important but often ignored detail is controlling the dough temperature. The temperature at which the dough is mixed and rises significantly affects yeast activity and gluten development. Einkorn dough works best in a slightly warmer environment, which helps activate the yeast. However, too much heat can speed up fermentation too much, leading to overproofing. To avoid this, using a thermometer to check the temperature of the ingredients and the surrounding proofing area is essential. Keeping these within the right temperature range can greatly improve the chances of successful einkorn baking.

Handling einkorn dough can be tricky, even for skilled bakers. The delicate gluten structure in einkorn flour requires a gentle touch, as too much kneading or rough shaping can cause the dough to lose its air and structure. This can result in baked goods that are too heavy and compact. The right technique involves being gentle and minimizing manipulation to keep the air pockets that are important for rising and texture.

The baking environment also plays a crucial role. Einkorn bread especially benefits from a humid oven during the first part of baking. This humidity helps with oven spring and stops the crust from forming too soon. You can create this humidity by adding steam to the oven at the beginning of the baking process. A simple way to do this is by placing a pan with hot water on the lower rack of the oven, which creates a steamy atmosphere that aids in rising and crust development.

Achieving the Ideal Rise in Einkorn Dough

Achieving the best rise in einkorn dough requires a clear understanding of the unique properties of einkorn flour and how it interacts with other ingredients and the environment. As an ancient grain, einkorn has specific challenges and rewards during baking, especially in leavening. Success depends on carefully balancing moisture, temperature, and fermentation time to suit einkorn's characteristics.

Hydration plays a crucial role in the rise of einkorn dough. Einkorn flour absorbs water more slowly than modern wheat flours, so it's important to approach hydration carefully. The dough needs enough moisture to activate yeast fermentation without becoming too wet, which can affect its structure. It's a good idea to start with a hydration ratio that's slightly higher than what you'd use for modern wheat flours, making small adjustments based on the dough's texture and the humidity in the air. Too much water can make the dough hard to shape, while too little can slow down yeast activity, leading to a dense crumb.

Temperature also greatly affects the fermentation of einkorn dough. The dough works best in a warm spot, ideally between 75°F and 78°F (24°C to 26°C), which promotes active yeast fermentation while reducing the risk of overproofing. Einkorn's gluten network is more delicate, and overproofed dough can collapse, resulting in dense baked goods. Using a proofing box or finding a warm place in the kitchen can help maintain this ideal temperature range.

Timing is another key factor in fermenting einkorn dough successfully. Generally, einkorn dough needs a longer fermentation time compared to doughs made with modern wheat flours. This extra time is vital for developing flavor and texture, as well as strengthening the gluten network. Trying to speed up the rising process with too much heat or not enough fermentation time can lead to underdeveloped flavors and poor texture. On the other hand, letting the dough rise for too long can exhaust the yeast's food sources, which can result in a lack of oven spring and a dense crumb.

To achieve the best rise with einkorn dough, bakers need to make careful adjustments and observations. Techniques should be tailored to the specific conditions in the kitchen and the ingredients used. Factors like the age and quality of the yeast, the grind size of the einkorn flour, and even the mineral content of the water can greatly affect the final result. Keeping detailed notes for each batch, including temperature, hydration levels, fermentation times, and the bread's texture and flavor, can offer helpful insights for future baking and help ensure consistent success with einkorn.

Chapter 8: Nutritional Insights of Einkorn

Einkorn Flour in a Balanced Diet

To effectively integrate einkorn flour into a balanced and nutritious diet, it's important to understand its unique nutritional makeup and how it works well with other foods. Einkorn flour is known for its high protein content, which includes a variety of amino acids that are essential for many body functions, such as repairing tissues and producing enzymes. Additionally, einkorn is rich in dietary fiber, which comes in both soluble and insoluble forms, each serving important roles. Soluble fiber can help regulate blood sugar and lower cholesterol, while insoluble fiber supports digestive health by promoting regular bowel movements. Einkorn also has a notable antioxidant profile, featuring significant amounts of compounds like lutein and zeaxanthin, which are carotenoids that help maintain eye health and may reduce the risk of age-related macular degeneration.

Einkorn flour stands out for its high mineral content, with more magnesium, iron, and zinc compared to regular wheat flours. Magnesium is important for many biochemical reactions, especially in energy use and DNA synthesis. Iron is essential for making hemoglobin and transporting oxygen in the body, while zinc supports the immune system and works with many enzymes. To improve iron absorption from einkorn, it's helpful to eat it with foods that are high in vitamin C, like citrus fruits or bell peppers, as vitamin C can make iron more accessible for the body.

The antioxidant properties of einkorn, due to its lutein and zeaxanthin content, become even stronger when paired with other antioxidant-rich foods. For example, berries have anthocyanins, nuts provide vitamin E, and dark leafy greens offer more carotenoids. These combinations can help create a balanced diet that reduces oxidative stress and inflammation, offering better protection against cell damage from free radicals.

The dietary fiber in einkorn is important for digestive health and can make you feel fuller, which is helpful for weight management. To get a good mix of both soluble and insoluble fibers, it's a good idea to pair einkorn meals with legumes, which are high in soluble fiber, as well as seeds and various vegetables. This way, you enhance the overall nutrition and support a healthy gut microbiome.

The gluten structure in einkorn is different and might be easier to digest for people with mild sensitivities to the gluten in modern wheat. However, those with gluten-related disorders should consult healthcare professionals before adding einkorn to their diet. For those who can eat einkorn, it's best to start slowly, watching for any reactions while enjoying the different flavors and textures it offers in cooking.

When substituting einkorn flour for regular flours in recipes, it's important to consider its unique hydration needs. Einkorn flour usually requires less water because of its lower gluten content, which affects how the dough feels and holds together. A smart approach is to start by replacing half of the flour in a recipe with einkorn and see how the texture and moisture change. This gradual method helps bakers and cooks adjust to einkorn's special qualities and achieve the desired results in their dishes.

Dietary Considerations for Einkorn Flour

To effectively incorporate einkorn flour into a balanced diet, it is important to understand its unique dietary features and how they relate to our bodies. Einkorn, an ancient grain, is known for its nutritional profile, which includes higher protein levels along with a variety of essential minerals and vitamins. The gluten in einkorn is quite different from that found in modern wheat, which affects how easy it is to digest and influences how we use it in meals.

Einkorn flour has less gluten than modern wheat flours, but it still contains gluten. People with celiac disease or severe gluten sensitivities should avoid einkorn because its gluten can cause negative reactions. On the other hand, those with non-celiac gluten sensitivity may find einkorn easier to digest due to its unique gluten structure. However, it's important to remember that everyone reacts differently. A wise approach is to start with small amounts of einkorn and closely watch for any reactions, like stomach discomfort or inflammation.

The high fiber content in einkorn flour is beneficial for digestive health as it helps promote regular bowel movements and supports a healthy gut. For those not used to a high-fiber diet, it's best to introduce einkorn gradually to avoid digestive issues like bloating or gas. Pairing einkorn with digestion-friendly foods, such as ginger or peppermint tea, can help soothe the digestive system and improve comfort.

Einkorn is also rich in vital minerals like magnesium, iron, and zinc, adding to its nutritional value. To get the most iron from einkorn, it's helpful to eat it with foods high in vitamin C, such as citrus fruits, bell peppers, or strawberries. This combination can increase iron absorption by converting it into a form that is easier for the body to use, which supports important functions like oxygen transport in the blood and energy production in cells.

When substituting einkorn flour for other flours in recipes, it's essential to consider its unique ability to absorb liquids. Einkorn takes in moisture more slowly than other flours, so adjustments in recipes may be necessary to get the right consistency for dough or batter. This property can also change the baking process, affecting the texture of the final product and possibly requiring longer cooking times. Bakers might need to try different amounts of liquid and tweak baking temperatures and times to work with einkorn's characteristics.

For those looking to add einkorn to their diet for its potential health benefits, such as a lower glycemic index compared to modern wheat, it's crucial to maintain a balanced and varied diet. Einkorn should be part of a diet that includes a wide range of fruits, vegetables, proteins, and healthy fats to ensure complete nutrition and support overall health and well-being.

Gluten Content in Einkorn

Einkorn, a grain with roots in ancient farming, stands out because of its unique gluten structure, which is quite different from the gluten in modern wheat like Triticum aestivum. The gluten in einkorn has less overall quantity and a different arrangement of gluten proteins, featuring variations in amino acid sequences and how the proteins fold. This special structure makes it easier to digest for some people, especially those with mild gluten sensitivities. However, einkorn is still not safe for people with celiac disease, as it contains gluten proteins that can cause harmful immune reactions.

The gluten network in einkorn mainly consists of two proteins: gliadin and glutenin. Gliadin is a single protein that helps dough stretch without breaking. Glutenin, on the other hand, is a larger protein that gives dough its elasticity, helping it keep its shape and resist changes. But because of the specific amounts and structure of these proteins in einkorn, the gluten network is weaker and less stable. This means that dough made with einkorn is less stretchy and can be denser and more fragile, unless special techniques are used during preparation.

When using einkorn in cooking, especially in baking, it's important to understand how its gluten properties affect the final product. Replacing all-purpose or whole wheat flour with einkorn flour requires careful adjustments in the amount of liquid, mixing times, and how the dough is handled. You might need to add more liquid to ensure the flour absorbs enough moisture, as einkorn flour tends to soak up more. Also, mixing should be timed precisely to avoid overworking the gluten network, which can lead to unwanted textures in the finished baked goods.

In addition to its gluten features, einkorn is also known for its excellent nutritional profile. It has higher protein levels, which can boost the nutritional value of foods made with einkorn flour. The grain is rich in phosphorus, an important mineral that plays a role in energy production and bone health. Einkorn also provides a good amount of vitamin B6, which is essential for making neurotransmitters and processing homocysteine. Plus, it contains beta-carotene, a precursor to vitamin A, which may offer antioxidant benefits. With its wide range of antioxidants and minerals, einkorn is a nutritionally beneficial choice compared to regular wheat flours.

Gluten Sensitivity and Einkorn

For individuals managing gluten sensitivity, incorporating **einkorn flour** into their diet can be a complex yet potentially helpful choice. Gluten sensitivity includes conditions like non-celiac gluten sensitivity (NCGS) and wheat allergy, both of which can cause different digestive issues and health concerns. Einkorn is an ancient grain with a history that goes back thousands of years. It has a different gluten composition compared to modern wheat, making it a unique option.

The gluten in einkorn has a simpler molecular structure, which might be easier on the digestive system. This is mainly because it has fewer specific gluten proteins, like gliadins and glutenins, that often cause negative reactions. It's important to note that gluten sensitivity is not the same as celiac disease, which is an autoimmune condition where eating any gluten, no matter the source, can lead to serious health problems. Since einkorn still contains gluten, it is not safe for people with celiac disease.

For those with NCGS, einkorn can be a possible substitute, but it requires a **methodical and closely supervised approach**. Starting with small amounts and slowly increasing the intake helps in checking how well someone tolerates it. It's important to watch for symptoms like stomach issues, bloating, or signs of allergic reactions. If any negative symptoms occur, stop eating it right away and consult a healthcare professional who specializes in dietary sensitivities.

Einkorn's **nutritional profile** also supports its potential use in a balanced diet. It is rich in important minerals like magnesium, zinc, and iron, and it provides a good amount of dietary fiber and antioxidants, which are beneficial for overall health. The grain's higher protein content, along with various helpful vitamins and minerals, highlights its nutritional value, making it more than just a gluten-related topic.

When replacing conventional wheat flours with einkorn, careful adjustments in hydration levels and handling methods are essential due to its different gluten structure. Recipes may need less water because einkorn absorbs less moisture, and the dough should be mixed gently to avoid overdeveloping the gluten, which can make baked goods denser. This process of trial and adaptation is crucial, as einkorn flour interacts with recipes in ways that can be quite different from standard flours.

Chapter 9: Expert Einkorn Cooking Tips

Enhancing Einkorn Flavor Profiles

To effectively bring out the rich flavors when cooking with einkorn, it's important to understand the grain's special taste and how it interacts with different ingredients. Einkorn has a unique nutty and slightly sweet flavor that works well in both savory and sweet dishes. Here are some techniques to enhance flavor when using einkorn flour:

1. **Toast the Flour**: Start by putting the einkorn flour in a dry, heavy skillet that's already heated over medium heat. Stir the flour constantly with a wooden spoon to avoid burning, and watch as the

color changes to a light golden brown. Continue toasting until the flour gives off a pleasant, nutty smell, which shows that deeper flavors are developing. This process boosts the flour's natural flavors, adding a toasted richness to baked goods or pasta.

2. **Hydration Matters**: Keep in mind that einkorn flour absorbs water differently than modern wheat flours. When making dough for bread or pasta, it's essential to let the mixture rest for at least 30 minutes to one hour after combining the flour with liquid. This resting time helps the dough absorb moisture, which improves its texture and allows the flavors of the grain to shine through in the final product.

3. **Use Quality Fats**: The type of fats you choose is very important for enhancing flavor. Pick high-quality fats like unsalted butter, cold-pressed extra-virgin olive oil, or unrefined coconut oil, as each offers its own unique taste. These fats help bring out the natural flavor of einkorn and add richness to pastries or depth to breads. Choosing the right fat can change the overall taste and feel of the dish, making it vital to select fats that work well with einkorn's flavors.

4. **Pair with Complementary Flavors**: Einkorn's nutty sweetness pairs nicely with ingredients that boost its flavor. For savory dishes, think about adding roasted garlic for a gentle sweetness, or caramelized onions for a rich, savory-sweet taste. Aged cheeses like Parmesan can add umami and saltiness, highlighting einkorn's flavors. In sweet recipes, spices like cinnamon, nutmeg, and vanilla extract can bring warmth and aromatic depth, enhancing the taste of einkorn-based desserts.

5. **Sourdough Fermentation**: Use a sourdough starter when making einkorn bread to take advantage of natural fermentation. This method improves the bread's digestibility by breaking down gluten and phytic acid and creates complex flavors that you can't achieve with commercial yeast. The fermentation adds tangy notes that balance out einkorn's natural sweetness, resulting in a rich and interesting flavor profile.

6. **Adjust Sweeteners**: When baking with einkorn, it's a good idea to reduce the amount of sugar or other sweeteners you normally use. Since einkorn is naturally sweet, using less added sugar allows its flavors to stand out more, creating a more authentic taste. This change not only highlights einkorn's unique flavor but also makes for a healthier, less sugary final product.

7. **Experiment with Spices and Herbs**: To further enhance einkorn's unique flavor, try different herbs and spices to find combinations that work well together. Fresh herbs like rosemary or thyme can add a fragrant aroma and earthy taste to einkorn bread, boosting its savory profile. For sweet treats, spices like cardamom or clove can introduce a subtle warmth and complexity, enriching the overall flavor and creating a memorable culinary experience.

Substituting Einkorn in Traditional Recipes

Substituting einkorn flour in traditional recipes requires a good understanding of its unique traits and how these traits interact with other ingredients. Einkorn flour comes from one of the oldest types of cultivated wheat and has a different gluten structure compared to modern wheat. This gluten is less elastic and more fragile, affecting how doughs and batters feel and behave. Einkorn flour also absorbs liquids differently, taking in less water than modern flours, which can change the moisture balance in your dishes. Additionally, einkorn flour adds a distinct flavor, with a mild nuttiness and a touch of sweetness, which can change the overall taste of what you're making. Here are some simple steps and things to keep in mind for successfully using einkorn flour in your recipes:

1. **Start with a Small Ratio**: Begin by replacing 25% to 50% of the all-purpose or whole wheat flour with einkorn flour. This gradual substitution helps you see how einkorn flour affects the texture and flavor without straying too far from the original recipe.

2. **Adjust Liquid Content**: Since einkorn flour absorbs less liquid, it's important to reduce the total liquid amount in your recipe by about 10-15%. This adjustment prevents excess moisture, which can make your final product dense or gummy.

3. **Mix Gently**: Because einkorn flour's gluten is more delicate, be careful when mixing. Overmixing can lead to a tough texture. Mix the ingredients just until combined, using gentle folding instead of vigorous kneading or beating to keep your baked goods tender.

4. **Monitor Baking Time**: Baked goods with einkorn flour often need less time in the oven. Check for doneness a few minutes earlier than the

original recipe suggests to avoid overbaking. This careful attention helps achieve the best texture and prevents dryness.

5. **Expect a Different Texture**: Using einkorn flour usually results in baked goods with a softer, more delicate crumb than those made with modern wheat. This is a natural feature of ancient grains, so expect this difference as part of the experience. The final product may not have the chewiness typical of modern wheat-based items but will offer its own unique texture.

6. **Appreciate the Flavor**: The nutty and slightly sweet flavor of einkorn flour can really boost a recipe's taste. It's good to choose recipes where this flavor will work well with the other ingredients. The unique taste of einkorn can add depth to your dish, making it a new culinary adventure.

7. **Experiment and Adjust**: Every recipe will react differently to einkorn flour, so be ready to experiment and tweak things. You might need several tries to get your favorite recipes just right with einkorn flour. Be open to changing ingredient amounts, mixing methods, and baking times to improve the final product.

Chapter 10: Creative Blends with Einkorn Flour

Mixing Einkorn with Other Ancient Grains

When you blend einkorn with other ancient grains, it's important to carefully balance their unique qualities to create a great mix of taste and nutrition. Here are some helpful techniques and tips for making these blends:

1. **Understand the Characteristics of Each Grain**: Take a close look at the properties of einkorn and the other grains you want to combine with it. Einkorn is known for having more protein, more fiber, and a wide range of nutrients, but its gluten structure is weaker than that of modern wheat. Other ancient grains, like spelt, kamut, or teff, each bring their own flavors, textures, and nutritional benefits. For instance, spelt adds a sweet, nutty flavor and has a stronger gluten network, which helps the dough hold together. Teff, on the other hand, has a mild, earthy taste and is rich in calcium, boosting the nutritional value of your blend.

2. **Consider the Gluten Content**: Einkorn has much less gluten strength compared to modern wheat, which affects the dough's texture and the final baked product. When you mix einkorn with grains that have more gluten, like spelt, the dough becomes easier to handle and has better structure. If you blend einkorn with gluten-free grains like teff or buckwheat, you'll need to make some adjustments to help the dough stick together. You can do this by adding binding agents like xanthan gum or by using more eggs in your recipe to improve cohesion and elasticity.

3. **Adjust Hydration Ratios**: Each grain absorbs water differently. Einkorn, in particular, absorbs less liquid than many others, so you need to be careful with your hydration levels. Start with a lower amount of liquid when you're making a blend, and gradually add more as needed. The dough should feel moist without being too sticky, ensuring it's easy to work with and has a good texture in the finished product.

4. **Experiment with Flavor Profiles**: The unique flavors of einkorn and other ancient grains can work well together. To create a richer, nuttier taste, try mixing einkorn with grains like amaranth or quinoa. For a lighter flavor, combine einkorn with millet or sorghum. Think about what you're making—whether it's bread, pastries, or pasta—and choose grains that will highlight the specific flavors of your dish.

5. **Test and Tweak Proportions**: Start experimenting with a small batch to see how the blend performs. A good starting point is a 50% einkorn flour to 50% other ancient grain flours ratio, adjusting as needed based on the specific grains and your desired results. Pay close attention to the texture of the dough and the flavor of the finished product, making changes to the proportions if necessary. Finding the right balance may take a few tries and careful observation.

6. **Record Your Results**: Keep detailed notes on the ratios, hydration levels, and results of each blend to improve your technique and ensure you can recreate successful mixes in the future. Write down any changes you make during the process and how they affect the final product, allowing for a more organized approach to refining and enhancing your blends.

Flavorful Einkorn and Grain Combinations

Crafting intricate and flavorful combinations using einkorn and other grains requires a good understanding of each grain's unique features and how these traits can be effectively used in cooking. Einkorn, known for its ancient origins, adds a special depth of flavor and many nutritional benefits, enhancing the overall complexity of a dish. When combined thoughtfully with other grains, the opportunities for creating rich, nutrient-packed, and tasty meals grow significantly. For health-conscious individuals aged 25 to 50, who enjoy cooking and come from diverse educational and cultural backgrounds, learning to blend einkorn with other grains can greatly improve their culinary experiences, catering to various dietary needs and preferences.

To effectively mix einkorn with grains like spelt, kamut, or gluten-free options such as buckwheat or quinoa, it's important to first assess the flavor profile of each grain. Einkorn has a subtly sweet and nutty taste that pairs well with the earthy and strong flavors of quinoa or the mild sweetness of spelt. For example, a balanced 50/50 blend of einkorn and spelt can create a flavorful and dense loaf of bread. On the other hand, mixing einkorn with buckwheat can provide a strong and complex base that's perfect for gluten-free pastries, adding richness to the overall culinary experience.

Understanding the texture outcomes of grain blending is also essential. Einkorn's gluten structure is weaker and less stretchy compared to modern wheat, which affects how baked goods hold together and rise. By pairing einkorn with a grain that has a stronger gluten structure, like spelt, the dough becomes easier to work with and results in a final product with a better crumb structure and texture. When using einkorn with gluten-free grains, you might need to make specific adjustments, such as adding a binding agent or changing the amount of eggs or water, to achieve the right dough consistency and stability.

Hydration is key to successfully creating these grain blends. Each grain absorbs water differently, and einkorn usually needs less liquid than others. It's best to start with a lower hydration level, adding more liquid gradually as needed to prevent a dough that is too wet or sticky, which helps ensure a smooth and workable dough. This method leads to baked goods with a nice texture and crumb.

Engaging in careful experimentation is vital to finding the perfect balance when blending einkorn with other grains. Running small, controlled trials helps determine the right ratios and necessary adjustments for hydration, binding, and flavor balance. Keeping detailed notes on these experiments, including the ratios used, any changes made, and the resulting textures and flavors of the final product, is incredibly helpful. This hands-on approach allows for refining techniques and can reveal delightful grain combinations that showcase the unique qualities of each ingredient.

Texture and Density with Einkorn Blends

Customizing the texture and density of your baked goods with einkorn blends requires a good understanding of how einkorn flour interacts with other grain flours. To get the texture and density you want, you need to carefully adjust the ratios of einkorn to other grains, manage the water levels, and control the mixing process. Here are some helpful strategies to guide you through this customization:

1. **Ratios of Einkorn to Other Grains**: If you want a denser texture in your baked goods, increase the amount of einkorn flour. This flour has less gluten, which makes for a more compact crumb. For a lighter and airier texture, use less einkorn and add grains with higher gluten content, like spelt or kamut, which help provide the structure needed for a better rise. Start with a basic ratio of 50:50 einkorn to other grains, and make small adjustments based on what you see, keeping track of the changes in texture and density each time.

2. **Hydration Levels**: Einkorn flour absorbs water differently, so it's important to manage hydration carefully. Because it has less gluten, einkorn usually needs about 25% less water than regular wheat flours. Start by using 75% of the liquid you would typically use with other flours. Gradually add more water in small amounts, feeling the dough to aim for a tacky texture that isn't too sticky. This fine-tuning is crucial for getting the right dough consistency, which affects the final product's crumb structure.

3. **Mixing Process**: Be careful when mixing einkorn dough to keep the delicate gluten network intact. Overmixing can break this fragile structure, leading to dense and heavy baked goods. Mix the dough just until the ingredients come together, making sure no dry flour pockets are left. Let the

dough rest afterward, which helps the flour absorb water fully and gently develops the gluten network. This resting period is key to getting the right texture without damaging the dough.

4. **Leavening Adjustments**: Because einkorn flour has a weaker gluten structure, it doesn't trap air as well as flours with stronger gluten networks. To make up for this, slightly increase the amount of leavening agents like baking powder or yeast. This is especially important in recipes where you want a lighter, airier texture, like cakes or bread. Keep an eye on the rise during proofing or baking to make sure the dough reaches the expected volume.

5. **Resting Time**: The resting time for einkorn dough or batter is very important for the final texture of your baked goods. A longer rest period allows the flour to hydrate completely and the gluten network to relax, leading to a more tender crumb. Time the resting period based on the specific recipe and the surroundings, adjusting as needed to get the best texture.

6. **Baking Adjustments**: Baked goods made with einkorn blends might bake differently than those made with regular wheat flours. Watch the baking process closely, and be ready to change baking times and temperatures. Use lower baking temperatures for longer periods to ensure the bake is thorough without burning the crust, which could negatively affect the appearance and texture.

7. **Experimentation and Notes**: Keep careful records of each baking attempt, noting the exact ratios of einkorn to other grains, hydration levels, mixing times, resting periods, and baking conditions. This detailed record-keeping is essential for improving your technique and systematically working toward the ideal texture and density in your baked goods. Analyze the results of each variation, using this information to make future adjustments and improvements.

Printed by Libri Plureos GmbH in Hamburg, Germany